Painting
in Public

Painting

in Public

BY

MAURICE GROSSER

1 9 4 8

NEW YORK · ALFRED A. KNOPF

⚜ THIS IS A BORZOI BOOK, ⚜
PUBLISHED BY ALFRED A. KNOPF, INC.

FIRST EDITION

Affectionately to my Mother and Father

Foreword

There is a gallery that attends anyone who paints in public. Its comments of admiration and dispraise beguile the artist at his work. One of the great pleasures of painting out of doors is listening to these observations. And if I have set down some of them as texts for my chapters, it is not at all in derision, but to record what the great public that does not buy pictures thinks of the mysterious art of painting.

ACKNOWLEDGMENTS

Without the help and encouragement of my friends Frank Daniel and Garrett Mattingly this book would not have been written or even begun. I should also like to thank Virgil Thomson for some invaluable criticism, Mary Schuster for checking my physics, Henry-Russell Hitchcock my architecture, and Chandler Post, Charles Arthur Lynch, and S. Foster Damon for similar kindnesses.

M. G.

Contents

Painting
in Public

Chapter I

PORTRAIT OF THE PAINTER

"Mister, is your name Artiss?"

(NEGRO CHILD, CHATTANOOGA)

A PAINTER in public, whether he is standing on a street corner in his oldest clothes and working at his trade, or in a drawing-room, clean, subdued, and on his guard, is always being asked to answer three very difficult questions. This is number one:

"Mr. Corot, it is so nice to meet a painter. I have a niece who paints too. She has never had a lesson in her life. But she does the most interesting things. She can make copies of Mickey Mouse so that you can't tell them from the original, and the girls she does out of *Vogue* are just lovely. I wish you would come out to see us and look at her work and tell us if you think she has any talent."

The answer I have for that one is very impolite. For I am answering, not what is asked, but what the questioner really has on his mind. I say that I do not give lessons.

The second question is more difficult.

"Mr. Rembrandt, I am told you paint. We have

some very valuable pictures at our home. My great-aunt Elsie brought them back from Europe with her, two very beautiful old masters. I know you love art. I am sure you would love to see them. We have had them hanging over the fireplace and they've got a little dirty, but they are still very beautiful. Last winter it was very cold and one of them fell down and got a hole punched in it, not a very big hole and not in a very important place. Now, I want you to come out to the house one day and clean the pictures for us and mend the hole and tell us how much you think they are worth."

That is a hard one, but I have found my answer. There is an excellent professional restorer at the art museum of a neighboring city. I give his name, say that he would do a better job of cleaning and mending than I could possibly do, that the museum is more competent than I to tell them the value of their pictures, for though I have often painted pictures, I have never yet been tempted to buy one. Then I escape if I can. Invariably before I get very far I encounter the third question. This is its general form:

"Oh, Mr. Landseer. So you are an artist. I just love art. But last winter we went to a place in New York called the Modern Museum. They had the strangest pictures on the walls, all circles and spots. They didn't make any sense at all; I couldn't even tell whether they were hung right side up. I am sure I could have painted some of them myself.

But I know they must be very valuable. Oh, Mr. Landseer, do you paint modern pictures?"

To that I always answer: "No, I paint contemporary pictures," or if the feed line is: "What do you think of modern art?" nothing is more useful than Gertrude Stein's "I like to look at it." Whereupon, if I can, I flee. In my professional life I am not a teacher, not a picture restorer or dealer or culture vendor. I am a painter. And I do not feel in the least obliged to try to remove that look of injury mingled with respect, of hurt confidence tempered by the love of art, that comes upon the faces of the public when it thinks of itself as looking at modern painting.

My answers are not fair. I know it as well as anybody. They are designed only to stop conversation and enable me to get away, to avoid getting myself involved in the laborious jobs of teaching, restoring, and lecturing, for which I am not at all prepared. Nevertheless, the questions themselves, and all the other questions they imply, are perfectly legitimate. And they are asked so often and so insistently that it is about time that someone actually practicing the profession of painting set about answering them.

Innumerable books have been written about painting as art. There is even one by Dr. Barnes of Philadelphia called *The Art in Painting*. But all these books are from the point of view of the consumer: the art collector, the art expert, the art publicizer, the educator, the museum director. They are mostly about judgment — how to tell true art from false — and the pictures on which this operation is so successfully performed are those which have been painted long ago, have already been sold, and now repose in some public or private collection. But, though the authors give plenty of excellent rules on how to judge art that has already been judged, there is very little in any of these books that could be applied to the judging of pictures that have yet not even been sold — a thing the reader most certainly must be able to do for himself if he expects anyone in the future to write about *his* collection. In short, the authors speak only of pictures that, by the employment of judgment and money, and by the passage of time, have already become art.

The painter is always more than a little embarrassed by the word "art." What he does, he thinks of as "painting." That is his inside view of the manufacturing process. The product, framed, exhibited, and sold, may later become art. But by that time it is a thing outside himself with which he is not at all familiar, for it is no longer a part of his private life. Of course, even the painter himself may eventually come to regard a picture of his, bought and paid for, put in a good frame, and hung on someone else's wall, as art, but only such a long time after he has painted it that he has forgotten how he did it, and could not possibly do it again. Consequently, art is a subject somewhat out of his province. But painting he knows all about.

He does it every day. And it is surprising that so little has been written from the inside by the painter himself to explain what his profession is like, and why and how pictures get made. For although Leonardo kept notes and Delacroix a journal, and Van Gogh wrote letters to his brother, all these are on the order of personal communications or private memoranda not intended for publication. As far as I know, there is no treatise on art as Painting.

Let us begin with a portrait of the artist.

The painting of pictures is an art — that is, it depends on highly individualized skill. It is even a fine art (a phrase, I have been told, Leonardo invented to distinguish his work from the work of everybody else), and the painter of pictures is an artist. But every artist is not a painter. He may be a writer, or an architect, or a sculptor, or a composer, or an executant of music, or an actor, or a dressmaker, or a surgeon, or a mathematician, or a cook. Most of these artists have different sorts of lives. Opera singers will live in apartments decorated like a box at the opera, all red and velvet and gold — it makes them feel at home. Sculptors will inhabit damp ground-floor studios where there are no stairs to impede the hauling of plaster casts, and where clay will not dry too fast. Actors live by night, painters by day, and poets any time they can. All this is natural. The different arts have different subject matters, different habits of work, different publics, and get paid for in different ways. There are, however, similarities among certain of them and when there are, their respective practitioners behave very much alike as well.

In purpose music and mathematics are in no way similar, the one providing, I am told, visceral, the other, intellectual pleasures. But the mathematician and the composer are very much alike indeed. Theirs are both sedentary occupations, and they are both likely to be extremely neat both in their persons and in all the other details of their living. The difference on paper between a B and a C sharp, or the presence or absence of an *n* subscript is to the eye slight but to the sense important, and this necessary meticulousness is generally carried over into private life. Both composers and mathematicians write hermetic and self-contained pieces, and are accustomed to address themselves to a small but extremely well organized public. Their work is very quickly known within the brotherhood, and very slowly, if at all, to the general public. Both devote a considerable part of their trade journals to the critical examination of each other's productions. They themselves educate the young of their professions and thus hand down the traditions of their orders direct and unimpaired. Both are usually found leading sheltered lives under academic auspices, their money coming more frequently from teaching or endowments than from a popular demand for their works.

The instrumentalist, the singer, the actor, and the surgeon can all be grouped together, and they generally understand one another very well. They all have a closer contact with the public than do the practitioners of other arts. Success to them is not a private satisfaction or a future fame, but an immediate and public reaction. Their success can be measured by applause. More than any one else they rely upon temperament and the ability to rise to the occasion. For their arts must be performed within a certain limit of time. During that limited time, which is also the time of their public appearance, they must be supermen. Before and after does not matter. In private they may moon around in bedraggled bathrobes and appear as half-witted as they please. No one sees them then. They exist only in public. So that the closer they approach the big time and the more complete the exploitation of their personalities is, the more exuberant become their personal appearances, the less interesting become their private lives, and the less fun they are to be left alone with. Because their usefulness to the public is easily judged, the pay for their services is easily apportioned, and they are generally found organized in unions or guilds for their mutual protection.

The sculptor, the landscape gardener, and the architect form another group. If there were an equal demand for their services they would all act alike. But there isn't, so they don't. All three work in the domain of public display and magnificence. But the architect has another field as well. He must provide comfort as well as grandeur, build homes as well as cathedrals, and here he can operate as a small manufacturer turning out a needed commodity. Consequently, the architect can be independent of the rich, of the corporations, and of the governmental bodies, as the sculptor and the landscape gardener cannot. But when the architect's clients are the rich and the powerful, he behaves like the sculptor and the landscape gardener. This is the pattern: if they are employed by the rich, all three do small works and develop a personal and characteristic style, a trade-mark that enables the client to know at a glance the name attached to the work he is buying. If they work for corporations or for the government, they have big commissions to execute, more than they can do unaided. Consequently, they must employ many assistants, hire large working quarters, and pay high rents; once the establishment is going, they must keep it going by getting other big commissions. As a result, they must cultivate a neutral style, at once pleasing to committees and not beyond the powers of their assistants to sustain.

The architect and the landscape gardener do not dress like the sculptor. The first two only draw their designs, a clean and sedentary occupation, and would never think of laying a brick or planting a tree. The ones you generally see are prosperous and have jobs and will dress as much like gentlemen as any other member of a country club. They have both gone to college. The sculptor, on the other hand, has probably not gone to college. A systematic knowledge of past styles is not useful to him as it is to them. And though he too wears tweeds, his are more likely to be of a liberal than of a scholastic cut. His hair will be wilder than theirs (an indication of his political sympathies), and his nails full of clay because he works with his hands. He is generally poorer and stronger than the others, more attentive to his own musculature and less to his respectability, and far more interested in a useful variety in his sex life.

Novelists and literary workers in general are ordinary citizens, occupying known places in the republic of universal literacy. It is they who, for the most part, constitute the intellectual world. They work in solitude, often at night when the house is quiet, and for their intellectual equals. Their public is voracious, their talent ferreted out by avid publishers, and their income relatively secure. For the printing presses must be fed. To this order, as an esteemed but less prosperous and little read subclass, belong the poets. These, during their youth (before they have ceased to be astonished by the subject), employ the most advanced techniques of assonance and association to write about love. The poets, along with the sculptors, are the chronically unemployed of the arts. For in the contemporary world the subject matters most natural to both — personal romanticism and the human nude —

however much appreciated in private, in public are now both extremely unfashionable.

The literary men with artistic pretensions, both the prose writer and the poet, have a characteristic that sets them apart from the ordinary citizen, and usually rather annoys him when he encounters it. Although they both use words as tools, the prose writer is easily persuaded that all words have fixed and universally accepted significations, while the poet believes that the intense personal connotations he himself has added to the meanings of certain words are actually what these words mean to everybody else. Consequently we all, at one time or another, find ourselves engaged in bitter disputes with them both — with the prose writer because, as laymen, we have used a word carelessly without due regard to its definition in the dictionary, and with the poets because we have used the word without knowing what the word meant to the poet. All this, making the private life of these workers quarrelsome and their love affairs dramatic, is not unuseful in supplying them with a subject matter in time of dearth. It is this that they think of as human relations.

Although in the strictest sense of the word the interior decorator is an artist, I did not include him among the artists, because for the most part he does not work like one. He is more of an agent, a go-between, a man who knows where things can be bought and what is to be had, a salesman for furniture, fabrics, and taste, and he lives very close to the manufacturers of these things. Although it might be supposed that he patronizes the painter as well, actually he never buys a picture. Partly because he knows nothing about pictures (he doesn't have to because his clients certainly know nothing about pictures either), partly because hand-painted oil paintings are expensive, and if clients want them they will prefer to spend the money themselves. Partly also because a picture of any force, originality, or value will, in spite of the decorator's best intentions, dominate any interior he can invent.

A good example of what the decorator tries to avoid is the painting of Matisse — so brilliant and overpowering that if one of his pictures is hung on a wall nothing else in the room can be seen. The only way to bring the room back into kilter is to counterbalance it with another Matisse, and then with a third. If you buy one Matisse, you become a collector. And for the decorator, a collector of pictures is a client lost.

Consequently, if the decorator cannot avoid using a picture, what he will select will be the most innocuous color print in the fanciest frame he can procure. The recent vogue of Marie Laurencin was a heaven-sent boon to him. Her colors are always charming and always the same. Her little girls without noses stay nicely on the wall, do not have to be looked at twice, and are not out of place in the frilliest of rooms. Because they are all alike, they can be used as an interchangeable unit in the mass production of interiors with a considerable saving, for the decorator, of both time and thought.

All the same, if one wishes to be charitable, one can overlook the decorator's uncritical dependence on fashion and his commercial associations — which after all are the necessary circumstances of his trade — and call him an artist of a sort. For he uses as his canvas his client's house, as his pigments the drapes and furniture his client can be persuaded to buy, and as his subject matter his client's aspirations. The purpose of his labors is to define becomingly and, if possible, to exalt his client's social standing.

Some people would also include among the artists the photographer and the journalist. I am sure they both consider that they belong there. At any rate, like the interior decorator, they admire the creative arts and feel most comfortable when they are somewhere in the neighborhood of them, where they can regard themselves as part of that inner circle. For just as the decorator likes to think of himself as an artist because he subsists upon taste, so the photographer believes that, although he does not know how to draw, he has nevertheless the soul and temperament of a painter, and the reporter on a daily paper imagines that in following the news he is on the road to writing the great American novel.

Painting and cooking are very much alike, but painters and cooks are not. Both arts employ a specialized sense and a manual dexterity for the gratification of a client. But although most painters like to cook (feeling a lavish irresponsibility in the mixing of condiments whose uneasy fellowship can at most produce an indigestion and not a ruined picture), they do not live or act like cooks. For the painter of our day is a free lance. He is not, like the cook, continually in the employment of one person or of one group. He is a pieceworker and an independent artisan. Consequently, he can have more regard for the rules of his art, for his personal tastes, and for his professional reputation than for the exigencies of any particular clientele.

In this respect, the painter is more like the doctor, who also seeks in his professional body protection from the exigencies of his patients. Doctors and painters understand one another very well. Doctors admire the painters' dexterity and intuition, which is very like their own. They buy paintings, accept paintings from painters in lieu of fees, and have painters as friends. Many paint as well. There is even held in most big cities an annual exhibition of paintings by physicians. The pictures, though seldom very original, are always surprisingly proficient. In fact, how sensitive the doctor is to the charms of the graphic arts can be told from a glance at the advertising literature he receives. On the adornment of their monthly circu-

lars and encomiums of cure-alls the big drug companies employ art work of a quality, freedom, and
advanced technique to be found nowhere else in
advertising.

Evidence of this kinship between the painter
and the doctor is that during the Middle Ages, in
Florence and in many other towns, the guild of
painters was included as a branch of the larger
guild of physicians and apothecaries, a fact that
helps to explain the surprising competence of the
medieval painters in botany and anatomy.

However, unlike both the doctor and the cook,
the painter no longer has any serious support from
his guild. He is a solitary worker. Unlike either
the physician or the *cordon bleu,* he must get his
training, not by systematized instruction in the
traditions directed by known masters of the art,
but in any way he can. More than either the doctor or the cook the painter must be robust and
have no serious bodily disabilities. He cannot afford to. His is by no means an indoor or a sedentary profession. If he paints out of doors, and most
painters do, he must be able to carry paints and
easel to the top of many a hill. Even indoors,
where painting is less athletic, he must walk miles
and miles back and forth between his subject and
his picture. For oil painting is practiced standing
and walking. Perhaps the painter grinds his own
colors. Most certainly he stretches his own canvases. And he does it all until he is quite old, until he must be brought before his landscape in a

carriage, until he must have a man to set up his easel for him and squeeze out his paints on his palette. Renoir's fingers grew so stiff in his old age that he could no longer hold his brushes. He was forced to strap them to his wrist and paint with a motion of the shoulder, but he still painted. And the vigorous old age of Titian is proverbial.

Titian is by no means the only one. A friend of mine, wandering in a New England thicket, came upon a little man on guard before a portable fence. Inside the enclosure sat an elderly gentleman busily painting at an easel. The little man stopped my friend and said: "If you please, do not approach any closer. This is the celebrated painter, Mr. John Singer Sargent. He is painting the view of Mount Monadnock." Whereupon Sargent stretched his palette toward his attendant and said: "An inch more of the blue, Rogers, if you please." Is this not an enviable old age?

A productive old age, at least, is not unusual for a painter. The active life he leads safeguards his health. His sight is good. Continually comparing objects with their image on his canvas exercises his eyes. Few painters, except the graphic artist who works close, wear glasses. Few, as well, have read a book. The painter is the illiterate of the arts. Nevertheless he is not uninstructed, for he has been trained, to some purpose, to see and to remember. If he has done any amount of figure painting, and most painters have, he can converse and charm, charm being the one thing that will

keep a sitter still. Mostly he paints by daylight;
his day is the sun's. (His week is the time it takes
him to finish a picture.) If he is working that
month, and even if he is not, he will leave a party
early by habit and try to get to bed by midnight.
For he wants to get up in the morning and paint;
painting is more fun than any party. When he
drinks to excess it is for personal or convivial, not
for professional, reasons. He does not have to use
drink or anything else to furnish him with subject matter or to arouse his emotions and excite
him to work. His emotions are not his subject matter. He paints, not with his soul (it is even doubtful if he has one), but with his eye and hand. So
he has a calm life and a long one and lives day by
day. Gertrude Stein used to say that the painter's
life is like this: he gets up in the morning, paints
until the light is bad, quarrels with his wife or
model, and then goes out to the café for a drink.
The painter's life is very much like that indeed.

The sculptor lives in the middle of his works,
walks around them by day, bumps into them by
night, and eventually comes to look up at them
and say: "I did that — it's pretty good," and himself grows firm and stolid and immovable like
his plaster casts. But pictures can be rolled up and
got out of the way. Some even get sold. The
painter does not have to look at them all the time.
He need not be awed by the grandeur of his own
talent. He can be an unassuming sort of person.
But he is not an intellectual giant. He does not

even belong to the intellectual world. He is just a man who has been trained to see, and the picture he makes is just a piece of furniture to be hung on a wall.

CHAPTER II

HIS PICTURES

"Of course he can paint good.
He's an artist. Artists can paint
better than almost anybody."

(LITTLE GIRL SPECTATOR)

To a world used to thinking of art as a cultivation of the sensibilities, the definition at the end of the previous chapter may seem coarse. Nevertheless, it is perfectly true. A picture is a piece of furniture. Its principal use is to adorn a wall. Its purpose is to give pleasure and to describe the visible world. It is made by a man whose hand and eye have been trained to the highest possible point of taste, precision, and skill. And though this picture may be used by the intellectual world to teach a lesson or to illustrate an abstract idea, it remains in itself nothing but an object made by hand.

In fact, painting, although it takes considerable intelligence to make it or to like it, does not belong to the intellectual world at all. The techniques of the intellectual world can mostly all be learned from books. On the contrary, painting can only be learned, just as cooking can only be learned, by watching somebody do it who knows how. The intellectual world is made up of things that can be adequately described in words, written down in books, catalogued in libraries, looked up by students, and used in tests. It has not much use for anything else, and the techniques that cannot be handled in this way are not a part of it. Its distinguishing characteristic is the printing press. By this earliest method of mass production any part of the intellectual world can be put out in a multiplicity of examples and at the disposition of anyone who knows the code. A book can be read by anyone who can read. A symphony score can be printed, distributed, and understood without performance by anyone who has had the proper training. A dress design can be stolen. Because all these — even the book, which is written as if it were intended to be read aloud — are plans for performance. The symphony score is silent. The dress design has no warmth. The picture, alone, is not a plan. It is in itself the performance. It is a unique performance belonging to someone. And the dissemination of a picture by all the color presses in the world will only serve to raise its resale value for the collector who owns it.

Pictures, of course, are frequently used by the intellectual world; the painter is called in to illustrate some idea for it. But the idea is only the reason the painter paints, not an integral part of the picture itself. A picture painted with proper skill and knowledge of the craft will last much longer than any idea it might illustrate. An idea seldom

remains alive and unchanged even for the space of
a generation. However touching the painter might
have been about the Immaculate Conception or
the class war, the sentiment he is celebrating soon
gets old and tired and thin and then invisible and
is gone, leaving behind nothing except what the
painter actually saw and put down. The Sistine
chapel once expounded a new and shocking system of theology. Now it is nude bodies. What El
Greco painted as Catholic devotion now tells of
Spanish elegance. Benozzo Gozzoli depicted for
the Medici the most touching of all Christian legends, the visit of the Wise Men to the Christ child.
Today his frescoes are about only what the painter
actually saw, the grave and morning-afterish
beauty of the Florentine young.

Nevertheless, there are certain pictures that, on
account of their great popular success, have been
taken over by the intellectual world as symbols,
and are now difficult to see as what they actually
are. But these are exceptions, the few times a picture has become a symbol that in turn can be replaced by a word. *September Morn* has a more
valid existence as an idea of modest exposure than
as paint on Paul Chabas's canvas. Marcel Duchamp's *Nude Descending a Staircase* has become to the popular mind the symbol of all cubist
painting. Raphael's *Sistine Madonna* must have
been the same kind of symbol for the early nineteenth century. For its writers attribute to this picture qualities that our present-day eyes cannot

find there, and which must, instead, be the attributes of some general idea like nobility or dignity, for which the picture had to them become a symbol. The *Mona Lisa* is a similar case. The enthusiastic prose of Walter Pater painted on her lips a smile that certainly was not there before. Since his time it has been as impossible for us to see her mouth without the smile, as it will be for our children to see her smile without the mustache drawn there more recently by the perhaps less-ecstatic pencil of Marcel Duchamp.[1]

Even in these few cases, it is the symbol imposed on the picture, and not the picture itself, that has become a part of the intellectual world. Even the most abstract picture in the world, say the *Nude* of Duchamp, is not actually a part of the intellectual world for the simple reason that the picture itself is not an abstraction. It is not the exposition of an idea that can be adequately described in words. It is not even a picture of the universal nude on all possible staircases. It is only a hand-painted oil painting belonging to Mr. Arensberg of Los Angeles, of extraordinary market value because nearly all painters agree that it is a masterpiece, because it is unique in the history of painting, and because it remains interesting to look at again and again.

[1] The last time I saw this print of *La Gioconda,* wearing its comment by Duchamp, framed exhibited, and offered for sale in a picture gallery, its price — $500 — excited considerably more public indignation than did its adornment.

A diagram in Euclid, to the contrary, does belong to the intellectual world. The diagram is an abstraction, the exposition of a general idea. The student is supposed to imagine that it has been drawn in all possible ways, with all possible sizes and angles and proportions. If the idea that is being expounded is really abstract, it is even better to have no diagram at all. Words are more general than any diagram can ever be. Something that can be adequately described in words does not have to be drawn. The diagram is only a crude way of making the important thing, which is the verbal exposition, a little clearer to the student. Consequently, in the old geometries there were no diagrams at all. They simply said: "From the line AB as a base . . ." and let the student figure it out for himself. The diagram took away from the generality of the proposition and made the student consider a particular case.

But the particular case is just what painting, even abstract painting, is about — about a unique set of visual relations that have nothing to do with words in any way. To take the simplest example: imagine that our painter has taken as a motif for a still life a bowl of apples. From where he is painting he sees a unique set of visual relations. The apples, the bowl, the light, the shadows, the positions and relations of everything make a unique setup. There is not another one like it in the universe. Out of that unique setup our painter composes his picture. If he moves his easel a foot to the left he has another point of view, another set of unique visual relations and another picture. If a fidgety visitor eats one of his apples the painter will be very angry indeed. Because then he will have on his hands a different set of unique visual relations and the subject for quite a different picture from the one he is painting. So that — and this is a general truth — painting is not part of the intellectual world at all. A picture is not an idea, or a lesson, or in any way a general statement. It is a unique piece of the most expensive furniture, made to be hung on a wall and looked at, and it is always about something a painter has once seen or imagined.

Consequently, the painter working at his trade is not expounding a philosophy or summing up the universe or rendering its guiding principles simpler to the mind. On the contrary, he is making the world more varied to the eye and adding, by delightful artifice, to its visible and material wealth. That piece of furniture the painter makes is one of the most luxurious and precious and permanent objects it is possible to possess. Objects made of noble materials do not endure. One of the late Roman emperors, voted by the senate his statue in gold, changed the order to a statue of brass, which he said would last better. But pictures are made of nothing at all. With a yard of cloth, some glue, chalk, oil, and colored powders, the painter creates a treasure, and once this treasure has been approved by his fellow painters (although it may temporarily go out of fashion), it never actually loses its value until it falls apart with decay. During the recent war when there was talk of the wealth of a European refugee, one admired not his bonds or jewels or platinum bullion molded into automobile tools to be smuggled across frontiers, but his collection of Renoirs. Hitler practiced the theft of pictures, as did Napoleon. England stole, or shall we say inherited, the Elgin Marbles. Italy has little farm land left and no forests. She has never had minerals. She is still rich in museums. The speculation in painting values alone provides the livelihood for an entire international trade — the picture dealers.

But the painter not only adds to our wealth; he sees, describes, invents, and civilizes the world as well. He is not alone. Music, literature, and other arts have the same office. Even the lowly detective stories do something of the same thing. That is why everybody reads them; not because our analytical minds need puzzles to solve (few readers try to guess the end), nor because we all hate our neighbor and delight to see him dead in effigy. If only to play fair and not confuse the reader, the detective story must place its crimes among credible people and in real places. Inspector French performs in a real English landscape (and how dull it is!). The London of Sherlock Holmes is the most convincing picture we have of London in the eighties. The Los Angeles region looks and feels and smells like Raymond Chandler's *The High Window* and *The Lady in the Lake,* and not at all like its image in the movies. (In fact, the movies usually refrain from picturing the real Hollywood at all for fear of dissipating its glamour.) To anyone who has lived there, the France of Inspector Maigret is of a heart-rending accuracy. It is the excellence of its descriptions and of its evocations of other places that makes the detective story so loved. It has become the literature, not of escape, but of travel.

Nevertheless, when a writer attempts to describe something he can do it only in terms the reader is already familiar with. An inhabitant of New York, told that New Mexico is mountainous, thinks of the Alleghenies. He cannot do otherwise if those are the only mountains he has seen. But New Mexico is nothing like that, and there is no way at all of telling him in words what it is like. For the writer can never make the reader see something he does not already know; he can only regroup in the reader's mind memory images that are already there. On the other hand, description is what the painter does best. He can present the image directly and not through the distorting glasses of a reader's memory, not in meager and imprecise metaphors but in actual re-creations of light and air and color and mass. The painter has been trained to see, and it is always a surprise, even to other painters, how accurate his seeing is. Provence looks like Cézanne's pictures of it, the

Bahamas like Winslow Homer's, the Île de France
like Monet's, and Paris, even today, like the pictures in the Carnavalet Museum that Hubert Robert painted of it in the eighteenth century. People who have been there say that Chinese landscape looks like Chinese painting (and I am sure
it does), and that Japan looks like Japanese prints.
Spanish noblemen must have looked like El Greco's portraits and later like Goya's. The Venetian
whores must have looked like Titians. Each valley has its dæmon, each race its type. The painter
puts them all down.

No one has ever seen anything at all until the
painter actually has invented it. Geometrical perspective was not a part of the people's vision until
the painters of the fifteenth century began to paint
it. It is not a part of people's vision today in the
two thirds of the world unaccustomed to the con-
ventions of Western painting. Objects probably
did not even look solid until painters showed
them that way. Shadows on snow did not learn to
be blue until around 1870, under the instruction of
the impressionists, although Leonardo knew about
it as early as 1500. To explain the paucity of color
words in the works of Homer, where even the sky
is not called blue, it has been supposed that the
Homeric man (like our contemporary dog) was
color-blind. However, if the Homeric Greeks were
color-blind, it is more likely to have been the result, not of defective vision, but of an incomplete

education and because the painter of those times with the few and probably dull pigments he had at his disposition had been unable to point out to his public which colors to see.

A whole literature of escape to the South Seas was built on the Polynesian beauty first seen by Gauguin in Tahiti. The Yankee whalers used to have a very good time there, and Melville even speaks of the natives as beautiful. But these island-ers were envisaged as classical, if dusky, nymphs, and not as the broad-faced and serene beauties whose actual appearance was such a disappoint-ment to our men in the Pacific area, brought up, as they were, on Dorothy Lamour. Even photog-raphers can only photograph things that resemble pictures they have seen. The concept they have in their minds of what a picture is, is, naturally enough, something a painter has once painted. Re-member how the early photographic portraits, with their even lighting concentrated on the face, their dark backgrounds, and their pyramidical compositions, resemble the painted portraits of the thirties and forties. The Civil War photo-graphs of Brady are modeled on the battle pic-tures he was familiar with. In our own day the photographs of Cartier-Bresson would be impos-sible without the paintings of Christian Bérard, of Eugène Berman, and of Pavel Tchelitchew. And the photographs of Walker Evans and his friends resemble in every way their model, the contempo-

rary school of painting that has for the last several
decades explored the tawdry picturesqueness of
the American slum.

The painter teaches everyone to see. His is the
first and most complete description of our ever-
changing world. He is a civilizing agent as well,
for description and civilization are almost the
same thing. Once an unknown thing has been described, it can be catalogued, compared with similar or different things, used, found again if lost,
replaced if destroyed. It is named. As every student of applied magic knows, to summon or cast
out a devil you must first name and thus limit
him. So now the devils are limited by being
named, they can be driven out, and the unknown
place or thing becomes part of the world we live
in. In fact, a civilization exists and functions and
continues in its own identity only in so far as it has
been described to itself and others. If a civilization
has been well described, it knows both what it is
and what it wants to continue to be, and it can educate its young with that model, its own description, in mind. That is why, in many ways, France
never changes, why, in the Emperor Julian's time,
Paris was already known as a center for perfumes
and furs, why the letters Mozart wrote from Paris
tell about the same people I have encountered
there myself. This continuance of tradition, this
civilization, is one of the things the painter can
help accomplish. And there have been no major
civilizations, at least none that we know of, that

have not had their poets, sculptors, and painters busy describing and recording what its people had on their minds.

Civilized places have always been well described. But in some of them the visual arts have been especially encouraged. Let us call such places the painting centers. It is there where the arts are taught, the market prices established, where there are more painters and sculptors at work than elsewhere. To the painting center the hinterland sends its young to learn art, its money to buy pictures. Everywhere else except the painting center, the painter thinks of as the provinces. For it is only in the painting center that communication between painters is good, and that all painters can know at once what is going on in painting. Athens was a center at one time for sculpture. Byzantium, Florence with its surrounding hill towns, the Netherlands, Venice, and Paris were centers for painting. Spain has always been a province. However fine Spanish pictures are, there were never enough painters painting in one place — six or seven major ones are not enough — and these painters themselves mostly learned to paint elsewhere. (El Greco learned to paint in Venice. Goya went to Rome at 23. Velásquez did not get to Italy until he was 30 and Zurbarán did not get there at all, but the masters of both learned their art abroad.) England has always been a province. Except for the work of a few, such as Reynolds,

Constable, and Turner, English painting has always been naïve, like Blake, or done by foreign
masters, like Holbein or Van Dyck, or under foreign influence, like Gainsborough. We ourselves
have always been a province, and all of our great
figures — Copley, Homer, Audubon, and the rest
— have been the outposts of the great European
tradition that, since Venice and the Netherlands,
has always centered around Paris.

A painting center is a place where much painting is bought and sold and where many painters
live and work — where there is a demand for all
kinds of painting. Consequently, in a painting
center the painter's training becomes complete and
he learns to do all the difficult things. Florence in
the fifteenth century was like that. If you wanted
to learn to paint (and a great many energetic
youngsters did — it was a good life), you were ap-
prenticed to a master, who taught you his trade
and sold your work as his own until you took
your examination and became yourself a member
of the guild. The examination consisted of painting a picture that met guild requirements. Guild
requirements were so high that even today the
word "masterpiece," which only means the picture by which you passed your entrance examination to the guild and got the right to be
called "master," is confused with the word "chef
d'oeuvre," which means the finest picture of all
your work.

In a painting center there was lots of competition, so you yourself had to know how to do everything. If there was something you did not know, you could easily learn it from someone who did. Lots of painting was sold and exported. The more painting was sold, the more the public was interested in painting. The more general interest there was in painting, the more painting got sold. The public interest aroused in painting spread to all the kindred fields, to a huge body of artists and artisans of all sorts — architects, furniture makers, dress designers, decorators, weavers, embroiderers, scene painters, gardeners, and so on, all profiting by the prosperity of the painter and utilizing his visual discoveries.

Most painting centers have been rich commercial cities. Perhaps the free and easy give and take of commerce is more congenial to the painter's necessary liberty of mind than is the stricter protocol of administration and government. However this may be, to become a painting center a city must, at any rate, begin by being rich. Florence was well-to-do before Giotto. She was conveniently located at the head of navigation of the Arno. She was a center for the wool trade. Her bankers had had the luck or foresight to side with the Pope in his quarrels. But many cities now are poor that once were rich. Money is a fugitive pigment. Art is its only fixative. The painters confirmed Florence's prosperity. Today, five centuries later, Florence has little wool trade. The Arno is no longer navigable. The papal bankers live in

New York. Nevertheless, Florence remains a rich
city. And had she been even more severely bombed
during the recent war, tourists would still visit her,
still admire and pay to see the memories of her
paintings and the standing walls of her ruins.
Paris, too, founded her prosperity on river traffic.
She will maintain it on painters. For when commerce declines, a city can remain prosperous and
remembered only in the measure that it was a cap-
ital of art.

There is a pretty example of how the painter
stimulates commerce in the way night clubs and
summer resorts follow his wanderings. Here, of
course, it is not the painter's visual knowledge and
his seeing eye, but his carefree night life and his
search for paintable landscape that opens up the
slums to the *viveurs* and the countryside to summer visitors.

The painter, along with the students of the
other arts, is likely to live in a poor section of
town. As Gertrude Stein remarked, when the light
goes bad he will wander out to the neighborhood
bistro for a drink. His working day is over. He has
not a care, for his conscience goes with the light.
Consequently, until it is time for him to go to bed,
he has a very pleasant evening indeed. The news
of his pleasures gets around and others come to
share them. Presently his low-rent district is filled
with night clubs, dance orchestras, "American"
bars, whores, pimps, and limousines. The rents go
up and the painter goes elsewhere. But he has left

behind him a night-club section. Montmartre was
started like that: in Picasso's youth there were actually painters living up on that hill. Later they
moved to the Montparnasse section. When I left
Paris in 1939 the night clubs had taken over Montparnasse and the painters were almost all gone.
Greenwich Village during the other war became
the home of painters who could not go abroad.
Now there are few painters left: the rents are too
high. But there is everything else one could possibly want at night. In New Orleans the other day,
I passed a bar packed to its gurgling gills with
music and the armed forces. It was named "Café
des Artistes."

When spring comes and it is warm enough to
work out of doors the painter goes to the country.
But he cannot go to just any country. It must be
a country where the landscape is both paintable
and habitable. He cannot camp on the edge of a
precipice for the view, or do pack-mule explora-
tions of the desert. Painting itself is hard enough
work without the extra complications of a difficult
home. As Degas said, painting is not a sport. The
painter must find himself a paintable landscape
adorned with a small hotel or farmhouse where
he can stay, and where the food is eatable and the
people friendly. He makes it his business to discover these amenities. Soon he is followed to his
retreat by other painters, and then by painting
students and people who like to live near the practice of the arts, and finally by the vacationist. So

that in the end, his "Landscape with Habitation," passing through the state of "Artist Colony," has become "Summer Resort."

However, this is only the painter's summer life. In the winter he goes home to a painting center. For it is there that painting can be done. A painter living alone in the provinces, away from his fellows, will be able to solve almost none of the major problems of painting. He will exploit a minor personal mannerism under the mistaken belief — uncorrected by the presence of other painters — that he is making technical discoveries. His painting will become what is known as "naïve" — detailed, precious, and overexplicative — precious because the exploitation of a personal mannerism is a form of self-indulgence, detailed and overexplicative because the painter is afraid that to his provincial public, which is unaccustomed to painting, what he is putting down might not be completely clear. The serious problems of painting he will not be able to attack, for they are too many and too hard for any one man, and their complete solution cannot even be attempted except in a painting center where there are traditional knowledge and many painters. Even there, the most difficult of all problems, the problem of the big picture, with landscape, architecture, still life, figures, animals, and a real subject, cannot be resolved without constant and continuous work at it by everybody. This big picture — this mural painting — is an expensive luxury. It costs more in time, money, training, and materials than all the other sorts of painting put together. Consequently, mural painting can be done successfully only in a rich world where there is a painting center. Mural painting flourished in Italy, not much in England or in our country. At times when there are not many painters around, or when the world gets poor, mural painting disappears. Or, if it must be done, it can only be done at all by using trick solutions to the painting problems instead of legitimate ones based on real experience — by substituting stylization for invention. And when you see on a wall great sweeps of smooth outline and cylindrical limbs in skin-tight clothes, you may be sure the painter was a lonely man or that his world was poor.

If in a poor world the painter cannot do murals, in a poor world the sculptor cannot do anything at all. In a poor world the painter still can paint. Painting materials do not cost much, pictures can be rolled up out of sight and out of the way, and the painter is not obliged to live in a fancy studio. But sculpture, even small sculpture, comes high. Sculpture (almost as much as the sculptor) occupies space, needs shelter, and must pay rent. With the few statues he and his fellows can afford to make, the sculptor cannot learn his trade. Just as no painter can solve a problem in one picture, no sculptor can solve a problem in one statue. Problems must be solved by doing them over and over again in all possible ways and different examples.

A poor world cannot afford all this statuary: the traditions of sculpture get lost almost at once. In our time Rodin was the last sculptor who knew how to do everything. Since his time sculpture has threatened to become stylized. In practice, stylization is a way of avoiding the major problem of seeing and of making visible to others what has been seen. It attempts, instead, the easier problems of neatness and of resemblance to models of past but still fashionable styles. Thus it is able to make the product seem more professional, less clumsy and unschooled, with a smaller expenditure of effort. To the outsider, stylization is apt to seem, like the royal marriages of Egypt, snobbery carried to the point of incest; nothing but art itself is good enough to fecundate the artist. We can only hope that both the act and the issue of such a union are more interesting than is generally supposed.

However, in a rich world where there is a painting center, neither the painter nor the sculptor faces this necessity. Both of them know their trades. The sculptor is not driven to stylization; what the painter can do on a small canvas he can do even better on a large wall. He does it over and over again, Giottos upon Cimabues, Mantegnas upon Masaccios, Signorellis upon Castagnos, as our bombs have discovered on the walls of many an Italian church. And since the live human skin is more interesting than the brightest surface of any dead machine, painting becomes all about people. Across the walls of public buildings and private homes, for all the world to see, parade the models and examples of human grace and dignity, and all the world does see and is ennobled by the discovery that mankind is an admirable race.

That is not now. Our world is not rich. Our necessities are difficult to get, our luxuries unobtainable. We talk a great deal of the luxury of our bathrooms and of our automobiles, forgetting that when the air is full of sulphurous acid and greasy soot, a bathtub is not a luxury, but a necessary instrument of health (Paris in the eighteenth century was muddy, but it was not black) and that with present-day city planning and congested transportation, to own an automobile is more important to most people than to own a bed. (Who has not seen, sitting beside the farmer's pathetic hovel, his black and shining car?) Leisure, quiet and easy communication, the necessary circumstances for creative work, are out of reach of all but a very few. Even the fruit of creative work is seldom available to us unless it has been deformed for mass appeal or standardized for mass consumption. Our foods are patent, our bread uneatable, our wine Coca-Cola. No one has any time because he must use it going elsewhere. We have for our church the movie palace, for our high altar the juke box, for our communion of saints the radio, and for our Holy Ghost the Voice of Experience. We live in a poor world indeed.

However, the world has not always been poor.

Nor will it always remain so. When the world
was rich, the bulwark of its civilization, the arbiter of its taste, the crown and preserver of its prosperity was the painter. He will be all of these
things again. I do not believe that even the painter
himself understands his own importance. It is
enormous. He sees for the whole world. Every
harmony of color, every pleasant shape you use every day is there because some painter once discovered it. Every grace of feature or form or gesture
you can see, you recognize because some painter
once pointed it out. And though it is God Himself
who is constantly inventing and re-creating the
world, it is the painter to whom He shows it first
and who delivers the new model to His public.

Chapter III

HIS SUBJECT MATTER

"If that paint is waterproof, how
much will you charge to paint
a pretty girl on my tire cover?"

(ALABAMA MOTORIST)

THERE is a curious phenomenon of modern times
that always surprises me when I encounter it. Ask
any educated layman to describe a painting to
you. He will tell you at great length about the
picture's composition, its style, its influence and
school, its color, manner, feeling. In the end he
will have told you everything there is to know
about the picture, except what it is a picture of.
That he may not even remember. But if you ask
a painter about a picture, he will tell you first of
all its subject. For the subject is what he himself
has on his mind when he paints his own picture.

There are very few things he can paint. He can
make a picture by painting inanimate objects, or a
view, or animals, or human beings with or without clothes, or a combination of any or all of
these things. These are the basic elements out of
which pictures are made: animate objects, inanimate objects, and landscape. There is nothing else.

But these basic pictorial elements are not the subject matter for the painter's picture. His subject matter is rather the anecdote he tells, the subject he discusses, the sentiment he depicts, with the infinite possible arrangements and treatments of this basic material. Consequently, there are more subject matters for painting than you can count. Anything will serve — theology, people, heaven and hell, kings, knights, gods and goddesses, the sea, battles, magic spells, patriotism, family life, theatrical scenery, Roman history, gems from the poets, elegance, fashion, grandeur, despair, sex, obscenity, satire, love, and so on, until we get to the subject not the least in importance today — the simple evocation of some other pictorial style.

The choice of subject matter is seldom the painter's right. Painters have clients who sometimes buy pictures. Consequently, the choice of subject matter is either made by an actual client or taken by the painter with a possible client in mind. Somebody orders a *Last Supper* or the painter thinks that a *Cow in Field* will sell. At times when the painter's training is complete, he does not much care what his subject is, so long as the final judgment of his part of the work is left to his own professional body. For, believe it or not, painters, malicious as they are likely to be about each other, actually know about painting. No one else does. And when professional judgment gets into the hands of a foreign group, like the womens' clubs, or a ring of dealers and critics, or the purveyors of soda-pop, very strange things indeed are likely to happen.

So the client chooses the subject and the painter executes it and everything is fine. But how good the execution will be depends a great deal on how seriously the subject matter can be taken by both the painter and the client. There are four possibilities.

If the client believes in the subject but the painter does not, no great harm can come of it. For although the painter will not have the patience to waste his best work on what he considers a shoddy idea, nevertheless he will find, to keep himself amused while he paints, as a parallel subject for his picture, a private joke at his client's expense. And although the picture will turn out full of sly jibes and references, it will nevertheless get painted. For there is nothing in the setup to keep the painter from painting a perfectly good picture. The subject has become a subject like any other, and the fact that it appears inane to the painter simply means that he does not take his client seriously. But his picture he can take as seriously as he will, and there is nothing at all to prevent his painting, and painting well, what he is actually at work at — a picture made up of animate objects, inanimate objects, and landscape.

If the painter and client both take the subject seriously, everything is for the best. Watteau once made a sign for the shop of his picture merchant. His merchant's intentions and his own were both

perfectly clear. Both actually liked and believed in
the merchandise for sale. The sign came out as one
of Watteau's best pictures. For he was able to employ on the adornment of the idea all his talent
and power and fancy.

This unity of intention on the part of the painter
and the client is a characteristic of all the times
that are known as the great periods of art. In such
times both the painter and the client believe in
the painter's subject and both work together to
make its explanation as clear and its execution as
worthy as they are able. Both the Greeks and their
sculptors believed that youth and the human body
were admirable in every way, and that the gods
are made in the image of man. Both the Chinese
and their artists believed that their gods were civilized beings. Everyone in the Western world up
to the time of the Reformation believed in the nobility of Christ and the dignity of His church. All
this is evident in all the art that these times produced.

If neither the painter nor the client can believe
in the subject, the picture will come out sketchy
or trite. Let us suppose that the advertising artist,
L. Fellows, so well known in the thirties, is asked
to paint a family of well-to-do Americans looking
as upper-class British as possible because they are
dressed in the garments for sale by the painter's
client — a manufacturer of men's wear. This
happy-but-horsy family is a fake. Both Fellows
and his client know it. Consequently, the painter

will have neither the patience nor the time, nor will he be paid enough, to employ on his picture the full resources of the art of painting, as Watteau could do before him. Neither will the client spend more money than he is obliged to, to have a silly picture, nor will the painter waste more time than he must to make one. The most elaborate picture a painter can produce under these circumstances is an engaging sketch if he is talented, or an imitation of yesterday's virtuoso painting style if he is not.

The worst situation of all occurs when the subject is one that the painter himself can take seriously but one in which the client himself does not believe. Now the painter is in a sorry fix indeed. He cannot deal with his client man to man. He cannot find out what his client actually has on his mind. For the client does not know what he wants; he is ordering, not what he himself would like, but what he hopes will please someone else — usually a public to whom he in his turn is selling something. In this case, it is impossible for the painter, through the barriers of his client's timidity and censorship, to have any real contact with that completely artificial construction which the client thinks of as the public. Consequently, the painter can have no freedom of movement. He must hold himself back. He cannot know how far he may go and not offend, just where he might tread on a gouty toe. He is afraid to paint according to his vision; he must play safe. He becomes

overcareful. Because he fears to give offense, he
timidly imitates some model that has pleased in
the past, and his work becomes spineless and over-
sweet. To replace the missing vigor he is likely to
employ the formulas supposed to give "strength"
— sharp angles and brutal lines — and to please
his uncertain client and his client's perplexing
public, the stylizations derived from a less devious
age. So that, if one thinks of the ecclesiastical art
of today, of our stained glass windows imitated
from Munich or from the Gothic, and of their
saints and angels with their inane faces, of the
shrines and altarpieces done in the most lugubri-
ous mingling of the neo-Byzantine and the neo-
modern, and if one remembers the marvels that
were done in the past to celebrate this august company of heaven, one is led to suspect that the art
ordered by the churches today is not so much for
the glory of God as for His publicity.

You see, the dangerous cases come when there is
doubt about the client's sincerity. This is the whole
problem of commercialism in art. It arises every
time the client does not know his own mind, or
when the painter must please a client who in turn
must please another. However, even in these difficult cases, from the client's point of view, the
job gets well enough done. Fellows's drawings
sell clothes. Quartier Saint-Sulpice saints can be
prayed to. Which is, after all, all that was intended, although perhaps not entirely satisfactory
from the point of view of art. Painting has always

been used for propaganda: the aggrandizement of kings, the glory of the church, the teaching of the rules of behavior — how to be good or pay taxes or what to buy. That use of the art offends nobody, as long as the painter is allowed to do his own job well, which is the discovery and the depiction of the visible world. But that job he cannot do if he cannot dominate his subject, if he stands in awe of his client, or if his client does not know his own mind. For then the painter cannot properly execute his picture. Either the painter is unable to use his full powers on his subject, or he tries too hard to please his client, or he simply goes blind. This is what is the matter with royal and millionaire portraits today. The painter no longer has support from his guild; his client's glory awes him; he is dazzled and cannot see. The portrait will come out bad in direct proportion to the social interval between the painter and his sitter. This social gap can almost be said to be the subject of the picture.

In former times there was not this difficulty. The client knew that a painter who was an accredited member of his guild was an authority on seeing — that what the painter saw was what the world looked like. Even the royal client submitted to this authority. And just as he now accepts the verdict of his physician, he generally accepted the portrait the painter made of him as a true resemblance — because the painter had behind him the support of his guild. If a client wished to re-

fuse a picture he had commissioned, if he was not
satisfied with a portrait he had ordered, the picture he questioned was first submitted to a court
made up of members of the painting profession.
If this guild court decided that the painting was
not up to guild standards, the client could refuse
to pay for it. If the guild decided that the work
was good, its decision would be upheld by the
civil courts. Thus the painter was protected against
the vagaries of a capricious client and was able to
face the most imposing sitter, not as an inferior
member of the sitter's own social class, but as a
man secure in his situation as master in a profession that was as absolute in its own domain as
any feudal aristocracy.

Nowadays, without the support of his guild, the
painter of the great is in a very uneasy seat. He
has all the excessive amiability of the insecure
guest. He must continually prove to himself and
to his client that they are social equals. Which of
course he cannot, for it is not necessarily true. The
only way he can save his pride is either to charge
so much money for his work that his client is impressed — in which case the painter is himself
awed by his prices and becomes overmeticulous,
or he must develop a contempt for the human
race in general and for clients in particular, in
which case the painter becomes an unhappy man.
One has only to compare a portrait by Titian and
one by de Lazlo to know that all this is true.

It is easier not to be awed by a client or impressed by a job when there are plenty of jobs around, and when the profession maintains its sovereignty by being itself the final judge of painting. (Imagine a doctor submitting an operation to a jury of patients!) But when jobs are few and painters quarrel and there is no guild support, any commission is an embarrassment. Almost any subject that is ordered is impressive, dazzling, disturbing to the painter's peace of mind; the fact that it has been ordered makes the painter more concerned with pleasing his client than with painting his picture, and the execution of his picture goes bad. What the painter needs is an undisturbing, an emotionally neutral subject matter, one that gives him no opportunity or temptation for pleasing, serious enough for him to be able to use on it all of his skill, important enough for any client to believe in, but a subject which neither the painter nor the client finds unduly impressive. With a subject of this sort, if he can find one, the painter's troubles are over, for then he can reduce all of his problems to the one he actually knows about — the problem of painting the essential pictorial elements — animate objects, inanimate objects, and landscape.

Now what is an undisturbing, a neutral, subject matter? Certainly not anything a client can order. For the purity of our clients' motives has become very suspect. The manufacturer does not believe in his product, the sitter wants to be made seductive. The Church no longer glorifies God. So

that neither the advertisement nor the portrait nor
the altarpiece offers a neutral subject matter. Here
are three subjects eliminated. A subject may be
neutral to the painter but not to the client, might
embarrass the client with innuendos or imperti-
nent references. So almost any picturization of
poetry or politics for private use is out. It might
involve the client in the participation in an out-
moded fashion or in the membership in an unfashionable party. Today's greater sexual liberty is
accompanied by a greater personal reticence. No
one wants to be compromised. So, gone as a subject is the nude — only to be hung on the wall if
it is an old master. In which case the emotions
aroused by the contemplation of its market value
outweigh the implications of its nakedness. Gone
too is the single clothed figure, the unnamed portrait. It might make someone suspect that the client had been to bed with the model and was presenting her, out of regard for public appearances,
in a more seemly, if perhaps less tempting, garb.
The landscape as a subject is still possible. But
only if it could not be supposed that the client had
been there on his vacation and had brought the
picture back as a touching souvenir of a pleasant
summer. The still life — bottles and candles and
books, all the paraphernalia of the school of Char-
din — is suspect. It smells too much of the academy. It might lead someone to suspect that the
owner of the picture had a friend who was an art
student. There are, however, other subjects for still

life — lilies, for instance, or apples and bananas (which, I have been told, are indeed its only basic subject matters). If our still life follows one or the other of these schools, if it suggests the organs of generation, and hence is impersonally scandalous and not personally involving, the most fastidious client can hang it on his wall without shame. For in this case the still life has become a part of the mythology of Freudian sex, which along with the evocation of the history of art, are now the only subject matters left in the world that are absolutely neutral to both painter and client.

Freudian symbolism can implicate no one. It is too generalized and too quaint, like the hell of Hieronymus Bosch, where no one can imagine himself going. The history of painting styles is also completely impersonal. It involves only an academic detachment, an Olympian evaluation of the past, and implies on the part of the client only cultivation and education, both honorific things. And although Freudian symbolism was originally employed with politically subversive intentions, and the history of painting styles has ended up in stock-market manipulations, as subjects neither compromises the buyer nor involves him in any party line. Both are reasonably pure. The one has become the subject of the surrealist, the other of the abstract picture. Neutral subject matter and modern art are almost the same thing.

I have not insisted enough on the difference between a subject that is neutral for the painter and one that is neutral for the client. A subject is neutral for the painter when it does not disturb his peace of mind, interfere with his seeing, or make more difficult (by emotional involvement, by promises of success or money, or in any other way at all) his depiction of the basic pictorial material — animate objects, inanimate objects, and landscape. A subject is neutral for the client when it does not compromise him, is not sexually or socially involving, and does not do any one of the numberless things that would render the picture unhangable or embarrassing to have around. In a picture painted today, if it is to be both well executed and acceptable, both neutralities are absolutely essential. Of older pictures, we do not require both. All that is necessary is that at the time the picture was painted, its subject shall have been neutral for the artist. Because a picture of a certain age, in a certain state of preservation, in the right frame, by a known master or school, may be a picture of anything and still be completely respectable. It is an Old Master. And its actual subject, which can cause only pleasure and envy and elation in the breast of the beholder, is how much money it is worth.

As you can see, subject matter is a very important thing to the painter, for it is its subject matter that enables the first sale of a picture to take place. And since it is from the first sale of his work that the painter derives his income, he is frequently tempted by the few subject matters, neutral or not, for which there is always a market.

I was once told, and it is perfectly true, that nobody who can play the piano or draw a likeness will ever starve. This minimal talent of the two professions assures a sort of livelihood. And in the same way, as far as painting is concerned, both portraiture and advertising offer the painter subject and subsidy. However, as I have already pointed out, both advertising and portraiture have lately fallen into disrepute and neither of them is as respectable or as well done as in former times, when the church bought the painter's allegories and the guild endorsed his portraits. Most painters, nevertheless, do a certain amount of either advertising or portraiture. But they are liable to get into trouble if they abandon neutral subject matter and the jury of their peers, to become advertising artists or portrait painters.

As I have pointed out before, advertisers do not really believe in the excellence of their products. The subjects they offer to painters are trivial. Nature as seen through an apple, or conviviality as seen through a *Last Supper,* is a serious enough subject to accept all the labor and skill and love a painter can use to adorn it. But Tutti-Frutti Ice Cream, as a subject, is both trivial and limiting. A trivial subject can only be treated in a frivolous manner. When the late Grant Wood elaborated with his astonishing technique and talent such trifling anecdotes as his picture of Parson Weems recounting the story of George Washington and the cherry tree — more what we are accustomed to see on the cover of the *New Yorker* than subjects worthy of so serious a painter — the results were lamentable. His talent overpowered his subjects. His labor rendered the jokes sad. The advertising artist, dealing with a more trivial subject than even these, dares not use more than part of his skill on his theme. He cannot allow himself to take it seriously. Besides, working as he does under a deadline, he has no time to. Mostly he works from memory and imagination, which is quicker and considerably easier for him than working from life. He cannot take time off to refresh himself by the study of nature any more than he can allow himself to vary his style. Because what he has for sale must be like what he has sold in the past. After seven or eight years of it, he is worn out and out of fashion. He never comes back in. And although while he is in fashion, his fabulous income tempts his fellow painters to do as he does, once he is out of fashion he cannot earn another penny and he is no longer even an artist.

The subject matter of a portrait is the resemblance. That is what is ordered by the sitter or his family. But everybody has a great many resemblances. His resemblance changes with every light and mood, according to whether he is in love or digesting his food, whether he is flushed with exercise or with wine, or is well or sleepy or ill. I am sometimes tempted to believe that the very bones of the skull themselves are flexible and change from day to day. Even a death mask or a cast taken from the living face is not a final, absolute resemblance. For the cast is taken from the supine head and the weight of the plaster pushes the flesh back toward the ears and gives a likeness that is drawn and tight. The two sides of any head are completely different in both proportion and expression. A slight change in hair-do or in make-up will change the accentuation of a face, emphasize different features, and consequently give a different resemblance. So the possible resemblances attached to one person are almost numberless and the one he chooses to recognize as his own depends on the fashions and admirations of the time and place he lives in, and has to do with how it is considered proper for someone in his situation in life to look and to feel.

Unfortunately, nowadays few sitters know which resemblance they want, and most are reluctant to accept the painter's choice. That makes the portrait painter's job a difficult one. It is easier for the photographer. He can offer for selection a number of proofs, all different likenesses of the same person. The sitter chooses the one he would like to resemble, and he actually believes he looks like that.

A sleuth in some early detective story must have said (for it has a Holmesian flavor): "The camera does not lie." But however truthful the camera may be in detective fiction, in life it does not see

the way that you and I do. Just as we ourselves
must learn to interpret children's drawings, which
are built on a system of perspective entirely different from the one we are accustomed to use, a sav-
age tribe unacquainted with the uses of photography must be taught to interpret the photographic
image. Our soldiers found this to be true when
they attempted to make natives of the Solomons
identify enemy ships from photographs. For the
camera sees in two dimensions, in a point-by-point
correspondence to the object, in a false perspective
engendered by the short focal length and wide visual angle of its lens, with an untrue translation of
colors into black and white and gray, and that in
a very limited range. It sees instantaneously —
only what is happening during the fraction of a
second when the shutter is open. If the camera is
loaded with color film, what comes out in the
photograph to correspond to the color of an object is a matter of complete chance. It depends on
the color process used, the length of exposure and
the method of development. And although in a
successful color photograph a green will sometimes photograph green, a red red, and a blue
blue, these will never be the green and the red
and the blue that the eye sees in the object, but
will be only pleasant enough symbols for these
colors, symbols that can never — even if a perfect
set of primary dyes were available — approach the
variety or intensity of the hues the eye perceives
in nature.

You and I, to the contrary, see with the memory as much as with the eye, in three dimensions, in colors that are accepted as what the real colors of the object are, in the perspective natural to a lens of very long focal length and very narrow visual angle. Our eye, moving swiftly and continually over the object, creates, with the aid of our memory, the impression of a very wide field of vision that we do not have at any one instant of time. Each time we see an object we superimpose the present image on all the other images of it that we have already stored up in our memory, and we see all the images at once. So that you and I use in our seeing a fourth, or time, dimension as well. The painter sees with his memory a little less than the citizen; part of his training as a painter has been to learn how to disassociate the image he is seeing now from the images he has seen in the past — to see with an "innocent" eye, only what he is actually looking at. If you consider all this, it becomes quite evident that the eye and the camera are not at all the same. What the painter sees — not what the camera sees — is what the world looks like. And contrary to popular opinion, a number of portraits of a person, done by different painters who all have the gift of portraiture, will differ less among themselves than a number of photographs of that person, taken by the same camera, but at different times.

The fact that the painter has been trained to see an object at the time when he is actually looking

at it is the cause of one of the difficulties a portrait
painter always has with his sitter's family. The
painter sees the sitter as he is now. The family remembers the sitter as he looked some time ago.
They still see him like that, and it is always a pain-
ful shock and a cause of dissatisfaction to them
how "old" his portrait looks. Later they invariably
say that the sitter has grown to look like his portrait, which only means that their stock of memories of what the sitter looked like has caught up
with yesterday's likeness, and now includes the
portrait. The fact that most people see with their
memory a great deal more than they suppose ex-
plains why any portrait painted from a photograph, especially of the dead, is always said to
bear such a surprising resemblance. Because memory fades, and the photograph remains and re-
places it. And the person is remembered, not as he
was at all, but like his photographic image. And
that anyone can copy.

If the painter knows what likeness his sitter
wants, his job is fairly easy. Great public and political figures know very well what they want to
look like. It is part of their business to know. It is
their trade-mark, their advertising slogan. It is
practically impossible to miss. Anybody can paint
it. I have never seen a portrait of Franklin D.
Roosevelt that I was not sure was a spitting image,
for all his portraits had the same resemblance. But
which resemblance the ordinary sitter wants to
think of as his own is much more difficult to di-

vine. However, there are fashions in resemblances
(such as how in Washington every man of a certain age manages to look like the current presi-
dent), and what the sitter wants to look like and
chooses to resemble is governed by fashion and
changes enormously with his time and his place
in society, as we can see in the portraits of other
times. How competent and busy were the English
lords and ladies of the time of Holbein! How
grand and self-contained were the French at the
court of Louis XIV! How good natured and
charming they were under Marie Antoinette!
How full-blooded and *terre-à-terre* they were as
citizens of the First Republic! Our own resemblances nowadays are less interesting. Hollywood
has imposed on us all the most insipid of likenesses. Everybody wants to look charming. Nothing could be duller for the painter. On the other
hand, from some photographs I have seen of the
celebrities of Mexico City, I should imagine the
fashion there to be somewhat different. A provocative and sensual insolence, combined with a certain Beethovian grandeur of soul, seems there to
be much in demand.

But all this — whether the sitter knows what he
wants to look like or not, or if he does know, which
likeness he demands — is a subject of painting like
any other, and more acceptable than most. The
danger to the painter is not there. It lies rather in
the fact that the construction of the likeness is itself a form of magic, and like any other form of

magic, very wearing on the person who constantly practices it. Getting a likeness has nothing to do with the technique of painting, even very little to do with the accurate representation in paint of the forms of the sitter's head. It is rather a form of caricature, of depicting character by accents. A person of strong character will make an interesting sitter, a beautiful but characterless person will not. People who know nothing at all about painting often do portraits quite well. Very good painters frequently cannot do them at all. It is a gift, a psychological trick, the result of establishing a certain sort of intimacy with the sitter, a form of magical domination. It is most certainly a magical relation. For if the sitter is ill or tired or has a cold, or comes drunk to the sitting, immediately his painted image will begin to look ill or wretched or tired or drunk, and do what he will, the painter cannot prevent it. No one can tell you how to get a likeness — even the man who has done it all his life. When the likeness is coming well, no wry color, no false stroke, will keep it out. If it is going badly, the greatest care will not save it. It is a fascinating game. The sitter loves it and never wants the picture finished. But it leaves the painter exhausted and fit for nothing. Almost any competent painter can turn you out a likeness from time to time, and most of them do. But the painter who paints only portraits wanders away into the realms of sympathy and magic, loses contact with the professional world and the respect of his fellows. And since once the likeness is caught, the portrait is finished and his job is done, the painter who only paints portraits ends by not being able to paint anything else.

Animate objects, inanimate objects, and landscape — this is the alphabet out of which any picture is made, and what the painter spells out with it depends on what client he has at the moment. But whether his client buys family portraits or dining-room pieces, history of art or art for selling, propaganda or pornography, saints or psychology, he is actually buying none of these things at all. He is buying instead the image of the world that the painter sees. And since every eye and mind and hand is different, and since the visible aspect of the world changes from day to day, and since the painter alone has learned to see it, the more commonplace and trite and comfortable his image will have seemed to the painter, the more extraordinary, shocking, and new will it appear to everybody else.

Chapter IV

HIS TRAINING

"There is a man in Rossville who can paint rings around you. But *he's* had lessons."

(YOUNG LADY IN ARKANSAS)

THERE is, and as far as I know there never has been, but one training for the painter. And that is drawing from the nude. Life-class drawing is the only thing that can be taught in school. It is, indeed, the only thing for which there is any proper schooling at all. And it is the one thing that, without exception, every painter learns. The naked human body is of all objects the most subtle and the most difficult to draw. The slightest mistake in its rendering is immediately apparent, even to the untrained. And it is, most certainly to the young and usually to everybody else, the most continuously and passionately interesting of all possible subjects for study, adding as it does, to the austerities of instruction, the luster of the human skin. The problem put to the student is that of delineating on a standard sheet of paper about eighteen by twenty-five inches in size, as accurately and as straightforwardly as he can, the forms and proportions of the model who is posed on a platform in the middle of the class. The figure is drawn as large as the paper will allow, and in charcoal, which is easy to erase and which completely lacks any misleading charm of tone. Charm or beauty of any sort is out of place. We are learning to draw, not trying to please, and the drawings are not to be sold. The models are of all sorts, but usually not pretty. The old and the fat ones are the best; being without any misleading beauty or charm, they are easier to see and to draw.

I myself was never completely satisfied with any of the life classes I attended. They were generally held at night; the light on the model was always like the lighting in the pictures of Caravaggio — strong and directly over the model's head. The neck and lower surfaces of the standing knee were always in shadow, so it was years before I understood how they were constructed. And the poses were never of the right length — twenty minutes, which was too short, or five days, which was too long. The lighting and the length of pose differ somewhat in different life classes, but it is in classes like these that I and every other painter for the last four hundred years, since the establishment by the Carracci of the academy at Bologna, have gone to school. Drawing from the nude in the life class corresponds, in learning to paint, to the study of the school fugue in learning to write music. Its rules are conventional and completely arbitrary. Its practice gives facility, ease in

making our lines and smudges explain on paper
the solid forms we are learning to see. And like
the school fugue, no matter how tenderly we may
remember it, it can never be used afterwards in
our professional living.

What we are doing is not making drawings, but
learning to see. It is a commonplace of the schools.
For anything that can be visualized in three dimensions can be drawn. ("If you are puzzled by a
form," says the instructor, pushing us up to the
model, "run your hand over it.") The amount of
skill necessary for signing your name will more
than serve for putting the thing down on paper.
And in learning to see we discover an entirely new
world, the painter's own, a world of three dimensions existing entirely in the present, where objects have form and color and situation in space
but no history, a world without snobbery, where
everything that is has the importancies of size and
shape and position, but not of good or bad repute,
where all things are morally equal and all have
solid forms and occupy space and can be walked
among and touched. We learn to see "pure," without the intrusion of words or symbols or memory,
to see only what the eye is seeing at that moment
and nothing more, to see, not in the convenient
shorthand of the word, but in the actual lines and
shapes and colors and forms whose concurrence
summons that word before the mind.

When we were children we were told that the
grass is green, that trees are green. As children we

were also told that there are three primary colors
— red, blue, and yellow — and that the complement of yellow is purple. All this is quite wrong.
There are any number of primary colors; what
they are depends on what pigments you have at
your disposal. And what colors are complements
depends on whether by color you mean pigments
or colored lights. If you mean pigments, then yellow and purple are complements, and mixed together in the proper proportions will make gray
(unless the pigment particles are practically
opaque, in which case they are not complements
at all, and their mixture will give a sort of red). If
you mean by color colored lights, then the complement of yellow is blue. Because if you mix a
yellow and a blue light, you will get a white light.
To the eye — for we see with light, not with pigments — yellow and blue are directly opposite
each other on the color circle. The colors between
yellow and blue on one side of the circle have
many names — orange, vermilion, red, scarlet, ma-
genta, fuchsia, violet, purple. On the other half of
the circle there are just as many colors. But we
have only one name for them all, which is green.
So to the beginner all these colors — one whole
side of the color circle — are equivalent to just one
word, and that word is equivalent to the paint in
just one tube. He paints trees green and the result
is appalling.

We were also told when we were children that
a hand has four fingers and a thumb, that a head

has a face and that a face has eyes, nose, and mouth. So the beginner will draw a head, perhaps quite well, and then he will write on it symbols for eyes, nose and mouth. And on the hand five fingers, and on the foot five toes. The result is very funny. But when he learns to see the features as they are, as forms and as the meeting places of planes, and learns to forget their names, he can draw them. Because learning to draw is the process of forgetting names, of unlearning, of acquiring an innocent eye.

That is drawing. That is the painter's complete schooling. For that is practically all his teachers can teach. But it is harder than it sounds. Everyone who wishes to paint must learn it. And the popular belief that it is no longer necessary to learn to draw to become an artist, that modern art got that way because the modern artists were unable to draw, is the exact contrary of the truth.

Drawing, painting, color, and composition are the four elements of a painter's training. The last three are most difficult. They cannot be learned in school. They cannot be got out of books. They are not for sale. They must be learned from doing, from watching one's friends, from the work of one's predecessors, from copying pictures in museums, from painting pictures oneself. That is why it is easier to learn to paint in a painting center like Paris, where there are thousands of painters practicing their trade, than in New York or London, where schools are perhaps better but painters few. It is notorious that English painters draw very well. But in France they paint prettier pictures.

To learn painting, one must learn about edges and about paint quality. Good paint quality is a great luxury. Normally, a surface painted in oil paint has a heavy and ugly appearance. Oil paint has none of the natural charm of gouache, fresco, tempera, or pastel. A whitewashed wall is more agreeable to the eye than any painted plank. To get a pretty paint surface in oil is not easy. It takes layers of paint, many of them, one on top of the other, a sensitive hand to lay them down, and time for them to ripen. As any householder who has ever painted a porch chair knows, one coat of paint will not cover. Even the most opaque pigments, like vermilion or white lead, are somewhat transparent when they are ground in oil, and become more transparent as they get older. When the picture is dry — after six months or a year — all the paint layers in the picture unite into one mass. One color can be seen a little through the layer of color on top of it, and that through a third. When you look at the picture you are looking down into the paint. The light has gone in, traveled around, and come back out to you reflected and filtered by the different pigment particles at all the different depths of the paint films.

The surface of the painting comes to life and the picture will change with every angle of view and with every change of light.

That is precisely what light does inside a rose petal. And that is one reason why with our brightest pigments we cannot imitate the color of a rose. If you extract the red pigment from a rose, it will turn out to be disappointingly dull and coppery. That brownish tinge is the surface reflection of the coloring matter itself. Almost every pigment has two colorations, depending on whether the light is going through the pigment or being reflected from its surface. Prussian blue powder looks bronze when it reflects the light, and gold leaf, looked through, is green. In the rose petal, however, there is little surface reflection. The pigment is in the cell walls, the light travels through them again and again. Each time more of the surface reflection is filtered out, and only the brightest red emerges to strike the eye.

This multiplicity of paint film is why no color print can possibly imitate a hand-painted oil, even if the paper is embossed, as I have seen in some beer signs, to imitate the strokes of the painter's brush. In a print the pigment is in the form of ink. It lies on the surface, has no depth, no life, does not move and change as does the painted picture. The colors themselves are aniline dyes, some not even lightproof. So if you still wish to consider yourself a patron of the arts because you once bought and hung on your walls a set of color reproductions, do not compare them with the originals. Your prints have faded long ago.

Consequently a print cannot be said to have a proper paint quality. In fact it cannot be said to possess a paint quality at all. And the most awkwardly painted oil is certain to have a less dead surface than the most perfect color reproduction. Just as there are any number of recipes for baking a light cake, there are any number of ways of producing a live paint surface in a hand-painted oil — by superimposing transparent or semiopaque glazes on a heavy underpainting, by a rough surface of opaque brushwork that is itself a light trap, and others. There are as many different sorts of paint quality as there are painters. But no matter what formula you use, the result will not be good paint quality unless your hand is light. And that cannot be taught. You must learn it yourself by doing and watching. Of course, good paint quality is not really necessary in a picture. Many a fine picture has been turned out with almost no charm of surface whatever: Frans Hals had very little of it. Many pictures acquire it with age. But good pictures do generally have a good paint quality. A fine painter, like a good cook, is likely to have a light hand.

Edges are much more important. If you can paint edges, you can paint anything. Edges, in fact, are so important, that the whole of Cézanne's painting technique was invented as a method of getting at them first. Edges are the lines on a can-

vas where things meet, where one form is in front
of another or in front of a background, where one
color abuts another. Varying the edges, losing and
finding them, soft edges contrasted with hard
ones, the presence or absence of outline, the mis-
placed outline, letting the light from a bright area
spread over the outline into a dark area, painting
the nearer edge on top of the farther one — all
these are the elements of drawing in paint, means
of creating depth and air and roundness. Edges
may be pulled as hard and as tight as piano wires,
as in Georgia O'Keeffe, or they may apparently be
completely absent, as in Claude Monet. But unless
the problem of edges is satisfactorily solved, the
painting is not a picture, it is a poster. Because a
hard unvaried outline lies on the surface of the
canvas and pins the forms there, allows no depth
or recession into the picture, and emphasizes the
flat pattern of the design. Whereas a varied outline, by creating a certain small confusion in the
eye as to the exact position of the objects in the
picture, allows them to retreat within the picture's
frame, and lets space and air into the picture.
Present-day mural painters often stylize their edges
and surround their figures with a sort of stiff wire
cable under the pretext of thus keeping their pictures flat on the wall. But I am of the opinion that
they are making a virtue of a necessity and would
not so treat their edges if they were skillful enough
to do otherwise.

A sense of color is good to have but not really indispensable. Many a fine painter has had just enough of a sense of color to set himself a rule-of-thumb color system and be able to stick to it (like painting in grays, with perhaps a spot of vermilion somewhere in the picture to make it "sing," or eliminating from his palette the dangerous colors such as the lakes or the violets or the bright greens). No student, however, can say that he has or has not a color sense until he can manipulate his paints without effort, until, automatically, his brush comes up from his palette with the color he wants, which he does not remember mixing at all — just as the pianist only has to think a C-major scale and there it is. Until then the beginner cannot know whether he has a color sense or not. He has not the means to find out. But even if he does not have one, a satisfactory enough color sense can be acquired. How quickly the troublesome distinctions of "warm" and "cold" colors resolve themselves into hitherto unsuspected tones of buff and orange, blue and lavender, which the student has actually learned to see! Practice and use do the trick.

The higher reaches of color, however, are beyond any but the most gifted. Any color placed beside any other color is distorted and changed. Their successful juggling is very hard to do. Delacroix said that he could paint the skin of a Venus using only mud from a ditch if he were allowed

to choose the surrounding tones. The felt on Van
Gogh's celebrated billiard table looks bright em-
erald green. It is actually a dull sulphur yellow. I
confess I do not know how it was done. I have
even thought that it might have been painted in a
fugitive pigment, Paris green, which has changed
color. But this is probably not so; that the table
appears the most brilliant green imaginable cannot be the result of an accident.

The curious optical illusions connected with
color can be very useful to the painter. The eye is
not a perfect optical instrument. A spot of red will
appear to it to be nearer than a spot of blue. Objects in a picture can be made to appear very solid
indeed by painting their retreating edges bluer
or "colder" and their nearer parts redder or
"warmer." It is possible to do this so subtly that
the spectator is not aware of any color change at
all. The illusion of air and space inside the picture can be got by spotting with different colors of
the same relative darkness. The eye becomes dazzled and cannot be certain how far away the spots
lie. Seurat and the pointillists made a system of
this, using quite large spots. But the thing itself
has been practiced, using smaller spots, ever since
painting first began. You will even find it in the
Græco-Egyptian funerary portraits.

There is another thing whose cause I do not
know and whose effect cannot be predicted.
Patches of different colors that match exactly in
relative darkness, neither appearing darker than

the other, at a distance of three feet from the eye, will often not match at all at twenty feet. Distance, as well, sometimes exaggerates quite small changes of relative darkness. These are perhaps the reasons why some pictures are incomprehensible at three feet and nevertheless read perfectly well from across the room, or will seem all right from close up, but spotty and ill-painted from farther away.

Artificial light from tungsten lamps, which is rich in yellow and poor in blue, completely changes the relation of the lights and darks in a picture. The yellow tones become lighter, the blue and violet tones darker. Some colors completely fade away. The brilliant Monastral green, a blue-green dye-pigment recently introduced, becomes twice again as brilliant, almost fluorescent, and is impossible to use if the picture is to be viewed by electric light. If the picture is painted in broken color (in the juxtaposition of spots of different colors that match in relative darkness), the spots will jump out like polka dots as soon as the light is turned on. If a picture is to be painted by electric light, or intended not to be seen except by it, the painter must leave off his palette the lemon yellows and the ultramarine blues, which become respectively almost completely white and black under tungsten light, and limit himself to a range of colors from orange to the blue-green of viridian. Fluorescent daylight tubes are even more tricky and distort colors even more erratically. For they

give the appearance of white light by the super-
position of a mercury vapor arc on a white light.
Under this illumination, any pigment that reflects
much light in one of the intense regions of the
mercury spectrum will appear much lighter, and
the ones that do not, darker. However, most painters very sensibly pay no attention to all of this.
Nor do they change their procedures to correspond with any system of artificial lighting, feeling that both they and the sun will continue to exist long after the disappearance of all these local
electrical contraptions.

Composition comes last on the list, and composition is the whole art of painting. It is the problem of filling the canvas interestingly, of holding
the spectator's attention by purely formal means.
Composition is what I think Clive Bell meant by
his equivocal "significant form." For composition
is why you can remember a picture and anything
you can remember is "significant." Attention to
the niceties of composition is why Audubon is a
great painter and Norman Rockwell is not. For
whereas Norman Rockwell devotes his incredible
skill for detail and drawing to the ornamentation
of an anecdote, Audubon devotes his equally
amazing skill to the clarification of a composition.
To a painter, composition is what a painting is
about. And he will labor for years on the same
composition, painting it and repainting it again
and again in any number of pictures. A spectator
need not know it is there, but a successful solu-

tion of the problem of composition is what makes
the picture work.

A composition may be flat or three dimensional,
lopsided or symmetrical, empty or crammed full.
But it must feel right to everybody. There are innumerable systems and formulas for doing it: the
Japanese occult balance — in which the full spaces
are balanced against the empty spaces; the early
German and Flemish system one finds in Dürer
and Schongauer — in which all the vertical and
horizontal and diagonal lines if continued through
meet at the frame and lead one into the other and
back into the picture; the "Greek" dynamic sym-
metry — in which the picture is contained in a
network of the proportions of the square roots of
two, three, or five, proportions that are supposed
to be the uniquely beautiful; the impressionists'
dictum that every square centimeter of the canvas
must be independently interesting; the theory of
the counterbalance of weights — that the masses
of the objects in the picture, like the weights on a
scale, must balance around some central point;
the theory of the pyramid — that the central forms
of a picture must resemble in their grouping that
most stable of objects; the theory of the circulation in space around a central axis; the theory
that composition is concerned with the empty
spaces between the objects and not with the objects themselves. (I remember a piece of sculpture
that was guaranteed by its maker to divide any
room in which it was placed into a pleasant com-

position.) There are many more systems of composition. They all work as long as they force the painter to watch intently the picture he is painting and to let the subject take care of itself.

A compositional system can be made on the basis of linear distortion. We all remember the optical illusion of the line that goes behind a pair of parallel lines at an angle and comes out apparently in the wrong place. Or of the two parallel lines that when they are crossed by other parallel hatchings appear bent. In the same way every line in a picture, even the edge of the frame, distorts and changes any line near it. The balance of these pressures and tensions can be used for balancing a composition. This was a favorite system of Cézanne's. In a picture the actual measurement is of no importance. It is the appearance that is the truth. To look straight, lines must be twisted out of place. That is why it is impossible for a painter to change radically any portion of his picture once the painting is well under way. He will never be able to get the distortions to balance again. It is much easier to start all over on a fresh canvas.

If a line goes behind a head of a portrait the whole head must be twisted and deformed. Otherwise it will not look right. Most of the Renaissance painters avoided the difficulty by painting behind the head of a figure a neutral space — a sky, a column, or simply black. Modern clothes, with their intricate V's of collar and lapel and the geometrical *décolletage* of evening gowns, render portraiture very difficult. For all the lines of the costume lead to the sternum or to the Adam's apple and away from the head. So that present-day painters prefer to dress their sitters in sport clothes, where these lines can be avoided, as they cannot be in our more formal attire. The ruff of other times made portraiture simpler. It isolated the head and offered it, as if on a platter, to the painter or to the headsman.

Geometrical perspective is no longer a serious part of the painter's training. At the time when the painter was principally occupied painting large pictures to be seen from a distance, perspective was very necessary. For the rules of classical perspective offer an invaluable framework for large and spacious compositions. Perspective, however, only works when the eye is considered as fixed and at some considerable distance from the object. Nowadays the painter usually paints small pictures and from close up, and the rules of perspective do not work at all. If we are near an object, the parallax — that is to say, the difference we see in an object's position against a background when we look at the object first shutting one eye and then the other, or when we look at it from a slightly different point of view — is very large. This means that when the painter paints from close up, he has two points of view — one for each eye — and two separate systems of perspective, and he must choose between the two for placing the lines on his canvas. Making the parallax even

larger by moving about a bit does not hurt. We
constantly move around; no one ever looks at anything with his eye glued to a peephole. Painting
with a shifting point of view will sometimes make
objects seem more convincing. Cézanne used this
shifting point of view a great deal. It was further
exploited in the early cubist paintings. Where objects lie in the picture is, for us today, more a matter of convenience and of composition than of any
exact rules of perspective. Indeed, perspective has
come to seem so odd today that the common type
of advertising drawing with parallel lines converg-
ing to a vanishing point is now identified by the
trade with what it thinks of as the oddest vagary
of all and is called the "surrealistic" style.

To a working painter all this division of his art
into categories of drawing, painting, color, and
composition is the bunk. These are convenient divisions for learning. But once learned, the separate compartments do not exist. To the practicing
painter, there is no such thing. He is not drawing
or painting or coloring or composing. He is making a picture. Nevertheless, for the student these
subjects are all real and must be learned somewhere. When our ideal painting center is operat-
ing, the schooling is ideal as well. There is much
painting to be done, more than the painter can
manage without help; he takes in youngsters as
aids and teaches them what he knows as quickly
as he can. They are being paid for it; he is relieved

of the tedium of the more mechanical parts. After a while the youngsters know as much as the master knows and they can set out for themselves. It is, you see, a circle; the more painting sold, the more painters; the more painters, the more competition; the more competition, the more interest there is in painting; and the more interest there is in painting, the more painting is sold. In the meanwhile the youngsters have become masters.

Today in a leaner world painting instruction is likely to be taken over by the academic bodies, the schools and colleges. They are pre-eminently unfitted for it. For they are capable of teaching only one thing that could not be learned more efficiently elsewhere — intercollegiate football. They import as a painting instructor a painter who, though he will have an enthusiastic student following, has nevertheless little academic standing. He is an instructor or an assistant at most, even though — poor man — he passes his vacations painting pictures he intends to submit as a thesis for a doctorate. (Imagine it, a Doctor of Oils!) He will have to teach, and in the end he will be fortunate if he does not actually come to believe in the academic doctrine of the equal value of all styles. Which is this:

To the scholastic mind nothing can be a subject for learning or scholarship until it is in a book in a library. No painting style can be thus embalmed until it is thoroughly and completely dead, until it is no longer startling or offensive, until it can

be easily recognized as a style of art, and until no
one has any reason ever to work in it again or any
ability to do so. So, to the scholastic mind, all
styles are equal; all the styles it knows are equally
dead, equally remote, and equally interesting. The
style of today, since it has not yet been put in a
book, it cannot know. This is an ominous thought
for any painter, still breathing the air and going
about his business, who has begun to receive serious attention from the professors.

The professor-painter takes a large point of
view, teaches his students to paint in all the styles
and tries it out himself. The things that he tells
them over and over again he must himself eventually come to believe. So he poisons his own mind
and undermines his own working ability. For creative work is done, not by being broad-minded
and understanding everything, but by keeping the
mind narrow and concentrating it on one problem, by doing that problem over and over again
and again. And by not believing, while one is at
it, that anything else is any good at all. (George
Moore said of James Joyce's *Ulysses,* "They tell me
he has written a book in a number of styles. That
can't be. Style is not variety. Style is monotony.")

The professor-painter has more than he can do.
He is an artist in a small town. Consequently, he
is the sole champion of the arts and must take up
arms in defense of painters whose work he personally detests. He is the emissary of the great

world of culture. Consequently just as the minister, the locum tenens for God, must preach in many a church, the professor-painter must speak before many a woman's club. He is the spokesman for the liberal point of view; he must defend the local labor unions. He is very busy. He is lucky if he is not made to paint the banners for the football games and the scenery for the dramatic society. What he teaches most easily in his classes is abstract art, that being now respectable on account of its supposedly more theoretical nature, its purer æsthetics, its distance from the vulgar and difficult necessity of drawing, and its rich relations who send it everywhere on tour, so nicely packed and well explained. He is surrounded by enthusiastic and talented students, who are with the greatest of difficulty restrained from entering upon a career for which there is not the slightest demand — their world being full of people who have such an admiration for Culture and for the Best that they would not think of buying and hanging on their walls anything but an example of the most internationally advertised art product. Which, of course, except in the form of a reproduction, they cannot afford.

A charming woman once said to me while I was painting: "My nephew used to do that. He drew and he drew and he drew, and he got so good at it that they gave him a job teaching. And now he doesn't have to draw any more."

The big art schools like the Art Students'
League of New York are much better than that.
They have painting and drawing from the model
with weekly or biweekly criticism by successful
working painters, who doubtless find their infre-
quent contact with youth stimulating and pleasant enough, and who are not forced to wear away
the edges of their energies uncovering buried talents or processing nonentity. The students have a
professional point of view; some even intend to
earn their living by the practice of painting and,
in fact, will. But all this is still not very satisfactory. There is no real necessity for anyone to teach
or to learn anything. No one is using any of it in
his actual living. The instructor is not using the
student's work; the student is not getting paid for
the work he does. So a great deal of time is wasted
in the lunchrooms in discussions about æsthetics
— which is mostly a sales talk invented by literary
men to promote their friends' pictures, and should
not concern the student or the working artist at
all.

Better than all this is studying painting in Paris.
There the schools are bad. But it does not matter,
for all your friends paint and sell pictures, and you
can learn from them. In Paris great reputations
are not impressive and no one is ever awed by
them, because the great live just around the corner, are seen every day, and can even be known if
there is any reason for it. There art criticism by
art critics is acknowledged venal, but art criticism

by fellow painters is sound. And no one ever utters a general æsthetic principle unless he knows from his own professional experience what he is talking about and is ready and willing to fight — as he often must — in its defense.

CHAPTER V

HIS TOOLS

"That's a mighty pretty picture
you're doing there, to be homemade."

(GEORGIA FARMER)

"So you sketch," says the hostess in a *Punch* drawing to her guest. "How nice. So much cheaper
than photography." And how right she is! Consider the photographer with his precious baggage:
his Leica and tripod, his lenses — Tessar, Dagor,
Contessa-Nettl (their very names evoke the fra-
grance of the camera, the poetry of the darkroom,
and perhaps some olive-skinned Graustarkian
beauty concealed within its labyrinth), his devel-
opers and enlargers, his Orthochromatic, his Pan-
chromatic plates, his Technicolor! ("See 'Up in
Mabel's Room,'" cries the movie ad, "in blushing
Technicolor.") How expensive it all sounds. And
how expensive it is. A sort of super-Meccano set,
adding set 5 to set 5a to make set number 6, but
whose divergent series, unlike the toys of my
youth, never reach a limit of possible acquisitions.
A fairy land of catalogues, golden dreams of Com-
pur, Duotar, and Voigtlander, of Contax and

Graflex and Minimax, of larger and longer lenses, of faster and more focal-plane shutters, of smaller and tastier cameras, all brighter and shinier, the one than the other — a jeweled paradise! What a poet was lost to verse the day he entered the portals of Kodak!

Yes, painting is much cheaper. All the equipment needed is a sturdy easel (mine cost a hundred francs in 1929 and I replaced it for ten dollars last year) and a light paint box with the palette inside. Across the easel and through the paint box flows a steady stream of canvas, paints, and brushes, all bought and used up and bought again with astonishing regularity — like the flow of food through an icebox. Painting materials are not cherished and hoarded, but used. No painter ever thinks of them as costing money. They are part of his normal living like rent or grocery bills. The paint tubes are emptied, thrown away, and replaced, the canvas unrolled, painted on, and sold or thrown away. Brushes are used and washed and used again until they are ragged and can be used no more. For a painter to let his brushes stay dirty is considered professionally immoral, like a child's throwing bread into the fire — the sure sign of an evil life. The painter thinks of none of these things as an expense. And indeed they are not. For pictures get sold and materials get paid for by the price the picture brings. Frames, on the other hand, because they are not in any way connected with the manufacturing of paintings, but are part of the external mechanism for turning paintings into art, the painter is apt to think of as a shocking extravagance. But what he spends on canvas, paints, or brushes he never regrets or even regards as money.

Most artisans treat their tools with respect. And, just as a good artisan can be known by his clean, sharp tools, neatly kept in proper order, there is a similar way for judging a painter. But it is not quite the same. Here I am disclosing a valuable trade secret, the infallible method of telling a good painter without ever seeing one of his pictures, from the simple inspection of the implements he uses — the pea for testing the princess. Examine his canvas. Look at his palette. If his canvas is the best and most beautiful that his money can buy and if his palette is filthy, he is a good painter. The canvas the good painter works on will always be costly and beautiful. For therein lies ease of work and the sensual pleasure of painting. Not so much can be said for his other tools. He may paint with porch paint from the five-and-ten, his solitary brush may resemble a pen picked up in a post office, and he may still be a good painter. When his palette gets overloaded with geological accretions of paint, he will perhaps clean it; when his paint box gets too full of leaves and dirt to close, he may chuck it away and get another. But the painter who wastes his sense of order and arrangement on his palette and paint box, will not have enough left over for his pictures. He is in love

with his tools, not their use. His painting will be
dry, thin, and economical, and he will come to no
good end.

You will notice that when I speak of painting
I mean oil painting on canvas. Because that is
what painting is today — not pastel, not tempera,
not fresco, not water color. "An amateur," Sam-
uel Butler has reported someone saying to him,
"can do very nice things in water colors. But oils
require genius." This is a very pretty sentiment,
not in any way true, but everybody believes it.
And because water color is also reputed to be
cheaper and less messy than oil (parents very wisely
give their children water colors to play with, because oils are with difficulty removed from rugs),
most beginners start painting in water color.

But nobody can. Not even the professionals,
much less the beginner. Water color is just too
hard to do, too precarious, too uncertain; far too
much must be left to chance. It is like trying to
keep house on a tightrope. And if anybody, by
some particular knack or uncommon virtuosity,
manages to learn to paint in water color, all his
water colors will look just like the water colors of
everybody else. They will be the same size, because it is too difficult to paint bigger or smaller —
the same texture, for they must all be done on
that same rough Whatman paper — in the same
manner, of Sargent and the school of impression-
ism that copies the shapes of the shadows in vir-

tuoso brushwork. And all of his water colors will
be landscapes, because portraits and figures and
even still lifes are much too hard to do in that
temperamental conglomeration of drip, sop, and
run. Worst of all, when the beginner has once
learned to paint in water color he can never learn
to paint in oil. He cannot train himself to be ex-
travagant enough with his paint or his time, or to
paint with thick lights and thin darks (which is
more or less normal in oil and precisely the opposite to what one must do in water color), or to
keep his picture light enough. Water color, naturally drying lighter, must be constantly painted
darker than one wants, but oils under the same
treatment become heavy and lumpy and black.
Consequently, it is very easy in any exhibition of
oil paintings to spot the painters who have the
habit of water color. Oil painters often use water
color for jotting down an idea or for planning a
composition, but they will never consider the result anything more than a sketch, however fine it
may be. Cézanne used to leave his water colors
behind him in the fields.

Oil painting is something else. It can be done in
all sizes, all colors, at all speeds, all times, fast or
slow, thick or thin, broad or detailed, rough or
smooth, matte or shiny. Oil colors are easy to
match, stay where you put them, work hand in
hand with you like a friend or mistress, and not
like a skittish house guest or visiting celebrity. Oil
is home folks. It is neat and exact, bright and easy.

It is a serious medium for serious work. Hurray for oil!

Before I go on about paints, I had better stop and give the reader a short lesson in physics, about the additive and subtractive mixtures of colors, and what the index of refraction of a medium does to the pigment ground in it. If the reader is not interested in physics, he can, with a clear conscience, skip the next few pages. For although the effects I speak of are real, and to the painter important, I can give for them only the explanation in fashion at the present time, in terms of the mythology of technological progress.

If you hold a piece of blue glass to the light, it will let through, not only the blue part of the light, but the green and violet part as well. All that blue glass keeps from your eye is the yellow and most of the red. In the same way a piece of yellow glass will let pass green and yellow and red and nothing else. Now, if you look through the two glasses superimposed, you will see green, for that is the only light that can pass both glasses. This is what is called a subtractive mixture of colors, and it is what happens when you mix paints if one or both of the pigments are transparent.

On the other hand, if you put the two glasses into two separate magic lanterns and project their two images on the same white screen, the red, yellow, and green parts of the spectrum, which are in the yellow beam, will fall upon the violet, blue, and green of the blue beam. All the colors of the spectrum will be mixed. If the glasses are properly balanced, the result will be a white light. This is what is called an additive mixture. It occurs whenever colors are mixed as lights and not as pigments. In subtractive mixtures — in mixtures of paints — the complement of yellow is purple and of green is red, as one well knows. But in additive mixtures — in the mixtures of lights — the complement of yellow is blue and of green is violet (or rather fuchsia). You can make an additive mixture by putting little dots of color side by side. At a certain distance from the dots, their images overlap on the retina of the eye and mix as lights. That is what the impressionists were doing with their spotting (later, pointillist) technique — mixing colors, not on the palette, but in the eye. Additive mixtures are more luminous than subtractive ones, so that by using all the brightest colors Monet was able to paint a luminous gray; just as by using all the orchestral timbres, Debussy was able, I have been told, to portray silence.

The existence of two different ways of mixing color may sound strange. But if you want to try it out, mix the dry powders of ultramarine blue and of burnt umber brown. If they are in the right proportions you will get a fairly bright purple. Add a little water and stir the mess and you will have a dark gray, almost black. You have changed your mixture from an additive to a subtractive one.

The "index of refraction" is the measure of how much a substance bends a ray of light that travels through it. It is the refraction of the glass it is made of, that causes a prism or a lens to deflect the light and form a rainbow or an image. Even an opaque thing, like a metal, has an index of refraction. The covering power of a paint depends on the ratio of the indexes of refraction of the pigment and of the medium in which it is ground. Chalk writes very well on a blackboard. Wet it and the writing disappears. The chalk itself has not been changed. It has only been immersed in water which has a higher index of refraction than air. The chalk has become transparent and no longer hides the blackboard. In the same way the opacity of a paint film will change if the index of refraction of the medium it is ground in changes. If the index increases, as that of linseed oil does with age, the paint film will become more transparent, darker, and richer. If it decreases, as does that of water color or tempera when it dries, the paint film will become more opaque, paler, and chalkier.

Oil paint is nothing but dry pigment powder mixed with linseed or poppy-seed oil. Many painters make their own oil paints just as they often prepare their own canvases. Homemade paint is less expensive and less likely to be adulterated than any paint you can buy. Oil paint has almost the same tone dry as wet, because its refractive index changes little on first drying. Consequently the painter working in oils has no trouble at all matching his wet and dry colors. However, the high refractive index of the oil renders the pigments somewhat transparent, and its yellow tinge dirties their tone, so that colors ground in oil, especially the blues, never have the beautiful intensity of the untempered pigments. A painter generally does not like to paint in too dark a key, because oil paint always gets darker as it gets older; its refractive index increases with age and the paint film becomes both richer and more transparent. This is why spots of retouching, put down to match the tones of a picture that has already darkened, grow darker still and become visible five or six years later as ugly discolorations, and why ghosts of the painter's abandoned intentions sometimes appear later on the surface of his picture — as in the celebrated Velásquez, where the horse has five legs.

Pastel is pure pigment powder, molded into sticks with just enough of a starch binder to keep the sticks from falling to pieces in the hands. There is no painting medium at all. Consequently pastel is extremely brilliant, as brilliant as the paint powders it is made from. The mixtures of pastels are additive — the small grains of dry color lie side by side like small dots. Blue and yellow pastels rubbed together make something that is nearer gray than green. To make green, one must have a green pastel. Purple, however, is not a real color — like orange or green, which correspond to certain parts of the spectrum. It is the name we give to the mixture of red and blue light, and can be properly got only by an additive mixture. So that purples in pastel are easy to mix and very pretty indeed, which cannot be said of them in oil. Pastel is very luminous, for like all additive mixtures, it reflects a great deal of light. Pictures executed in it are just as permanent as the pigments used and the paper they are on, provided they are protected from damp and rubbing. The pastels by La Tour are probably less changed than any of the oils of the other eighteenth-century portraitists. There used to be in Naples a contemporary copy of Velásquez's *Bacchus and the Vintagers* that is perhaps more brilliant than the original ever was. But pastel is in infinitely more danger of accidents than is oil, and is just as hard to work with. To protect it, a pastel must be framed under glass at once; and no one wants his studio cluttered up with a lot of glass and framed pictures. Pastel can be fixed, of course, by spraying something on it, like gum or a thin varnish. Degas must have used some such system. But whatever is used kills the brilliance of the pastel — and its reason for being. For portraits, pastel has this advantage — when it is done it is done. This is not true for an oil picture. It takes a certain time for an oil painting to ripen, for the colors to blend, for the separate layers to become unified, for the paint to become richer by the increase of the index of refraction of the oil. It is always embar-

rassing to have to turn over to a client something
that looks unfinished, chalky, and dead, and tell
him that in six months everything will be all
right. It is true, but he won't believe you. Pastel,
on the other hand, does not have to wait. The last
stroke completes it.

Tempera is perhaps the most beautiful of all the
ways of painting. There are any number of tem-
peras. Many are trade secrets, studio secrets, or
lost. Many are down in books. In general, tempera is a mayonnaise sauce (technically an emul-
sion) made with egg, oil, and varnish, and thinned
with water. But practically any household commodity — wax, milk, flour, lye, vinegar, honey,
cherry gum, fig milk, and so on — has gone into
the composition of one of them. Because water
thins it, a tempera medium was indispensable before the commercial distillation of turpentine
made oil painting practical. Because the medium
has no color (the egg yellow bleaches out after a
few days) and once it is dry, both an unchanging
refractive index and enormous physical strength,
colors ground in it are very brilliant, do not change
with age, and actually protect the surface they are
painted on. However, the change in the refractive
index of the medium from the wet state to the
dry is very great. And since this happens almost
at once, with the evaporation of the water, and in
a very irregular manner, the matching of colors
in tempera is very difficult and modeling in paint
is almost impossible. For modeling, one is forced

to use crosshatching and drawing strokes. Tempera, to be sure, is often used nowadays as a first coat for rapidly laying in an oil picture. Or, mixed up in little pots in a prearranged color scale, it is employed on plaster panels by people of an archæological mind — generally trained in Florence — in what they consider the cinquecento manner. Indeed, a tempera paint surface is so beautiful that in spite of the difficulty of its employment, it is nevertheless very tempting to the painter.

Fresco has about disappeared from the modern world along with its only reason for existence, mural painting. It is, to my way of thinking, the most difficult of all the painting techniques. The pigment, ground in water and without the addition of a binder of any sort, is painted into the fresh plaster of a plaster wall. Only the earth colors and a few others that the lime does not affect can be used. The lakes, vermilion, and ultramarine, must be discarded. Slaked lime is used for white. The setting of the plaster incorporates the colors into its surface. One can tell by counting the joints of a fresco, exactly how many days the painter worked on it. For he must paint the picture in small sections. Only the area which can be finished before the plaster dries — in six or seven hours at the most — can be prepared. And retouching is not possible. The colors dry pale. All the tones must be mixed in advance. Once they are dry on the wall, it is impossible to match them. Nevertheless, in spite of its difficulty, fresco was practiced at one time with extraordinary skill and ease. And I, for one, cannot imagine anything more beautiful then the Benozzo Gozzoli room in Florence. Fresco stands very ill the damp and smoke of our northern cities, but it is much practiced in Mexico, where the climate and the public taste are evidently drier and purer than our own.

Of course, mural painting does not necessarily have to be done in fresco, and today seldom is. The difficulties of the medium are usually too great to be faced. Ordinarily in modern times the mural is painted in oil on canvas in the painter's studio and is then pasted to the wall it is intended to adorn by a member of the painters' and paperhangers' union; there it cannot be retouched by the painter unless he is a member of that union himself. There was practiced in Roman times a mysterious method of encaustic painting in which the colors were presumably mixed with melted wax and applied hot. *The Last Supper* of Leonardo was done in some elaborate and secret process of oil or wax or tempera invented by the painter, and is rather an example of literary immortality than of the permanence of paint. For the picture had already begun to deteriorate before the painter had finished it, and by the time it was defaced by Napoleon's horses, it had, I understand, already been repainted several times. It was again repainted in the 1900's by a German professor, and now, after its recent redestruction, will again be repainted, presumably this time by a member of one of our allied nations.[1]

Modern painting methods have, in fact, very little at all in common with those of the past. If you have ever stood in a museum and watched a painter copying an old master, you will certainly be aware of this. For you cannot have failed to notice how little the painter's copy is ever like his model. That is not surprising. He is not using the same sort of paint.

If, until about the year 1830, you had gone to a color merchant's to buy paint, you would have come away, not with paint already prepared, but with dry pigment in powder or lumps, and you or your apprentice would have made paint out of it at home. You would have ground it with linseed oil, or glue, or egg, or with mixtures that were secrets, or recipes of common knowledge that now are lost because no one ever thought of writing them down. And you would have used the paint as you made it. For if you did not, it dried up.

Eventually, color merchants began to mix paint for the painters. Prepared paint was sold, stored in little bladders or little parchment bags with a brass nozzle, or simply with a thumb tack stuck in to make and close the hole. Containers of this sort

[1] This has now been done, and the picture is again, through the courtesy of the Allied Art Commission, in a perfect state of preservation.

were neither cheap nor practical. With the invention of the tin tube (according to Winsor and Newton, the English color merchants, it came on the market in 1841), a great change took place.

The painter was now completely freed of the necessity of grinding his own paint. Paints could be kept a long time without drying up. Painting kits became compact and light and could be carried anywhere. Landscape began to be painted on the spot, and not, as it had always been done before, in the studio from sketches. Color merchants became paint manufacturers. To keep their paints from drying up on the shelf before they were sold, they began to add wax and insoluble metallic soaps to their mixtures. These additions — aluminum or magnesium stearates and palmitates, or hydrates of alumina and silica and so on — transparent, cheap, and highly absorbent of oil, gave oil paint an entirely new texture. Painters began to paint in a rough-surfaced impasto, the thicker substance of the paint standing up on the canvas like little pats of butter. It actually took more and thicker paint to cover a canvas, for the adulterant enabled the color merchant to put more oil and less pigment in his mixtures, and the paints were less opaque than before. The picture might dry up in spots and lighten in spots. To correct this, heavy and quick varnishing became necessary. The elaborate impressionist technique of interlocking brush strokes of the brightest colors was probably invented to enable the painter to get with these store-bought colors as rich a surface as the ancients were able to obtain with their fewer pigments and their paints prepared at home.

Our chemists have presented us with many new and brilliant pigments unknown to the old masters. Where they had two yellows, both dull, and vermilion, we have a complete scale of the cadmiums from the palest lemon to a middle red. Where they possessed a real ultramarine (extracted from crushed lapis lazuli, permanent, but costing its weight in solid gold), a fugitive indigo, and a doubtful azurite, we have cerulean, monastral, and cobalt. We have bright and permanent greens; they had none. Their lakes were perhaps superior to our alizarin crimson. But that may have been a skill in handling as well as a lost secret of preparation. What both we and they lack is in the range from red through the rosy tones to purple. The painting of red and violet flowers, if we wish to equal their hues, cannot be done — not until some friendly chemist finds for us some really intense, permanent, unbleeding rosy-reds, both transparent and opaque. Of course, we can get along very well without them. And we do. But pigments like that would be a great pleasure to possess.

There is nothing mysterious about the actual pigments used in the old paintings. They have all been analyzed by chemistry. But how they were painted and in precisely what medium are more difficult to discover. Rabbit-skin glue and gelatin

are probably precisely the same in a chemical analysis. Nevertheless, they do not act at all the same
way in priming a canvas. I doubt that even the
best of chemists could tell me why the mayonnaise
sauce, so easy to make in America, seems to be one
of the most difficult of all culinary feats in France.
Processes of cookery are almost impossible to re-
construct from an inspection of the product. And
cooking recipes are exactly what the secrets of the
old masters were. There are in Dürer a yellow and
a green that, I am told, can only be saffron and
verdigris, two notoriously fugitive pigments. There
is some vague report of using them with, or boil-
ing them in, Venice turpentine, an exudation of
the spruce. However that may be, the colors are
as bright today as the day Dürer put them on. Nobody knows how or why. There is even a possi-
bility that the celebrated "brown tree" of the eighteenth-century landscapes comes from a tree that
was originally intended to be green, but that,
painted in verdigris after the secret had been lost,
turned brown, and, as a brown tree, became a fashion because it was pretty that way. Cennino Cen-
nini, writing a painting manual in the early fifteenth century, left elaborate instructions for the
painting of pictures in egg tempera. I would defy
the most skillful painter to copy, by the methods
he describes, a Filippino Lippi, who also painted in
egg tempera. Nearer to us there is in New York a
portrait of Maria Anna of Austria by Velásquez
painted, as it would seem, in only vermilion, um-

ber, black, and white. The most astute copyist in the world could not imitate its silvery grays and flesh tones using boughten tubes of only those colors. I doubt whether he could do it using all the colors in the modern palette. There is, or was, in the Fogg Museum in Cambridge, an unfinished Tintoretto in which the flesh of the goddess, cool and matte, seems to have been dusted and smoothed with some heavenly and most ambrosial cosmetic. I and any other painter would give our right hands to be able to paint it. For it cannot be accomplished with anything we have in our paint boxes.

Of course, we can always console ourselves with the thought that the paint qualities of the old masters are an effect of time, and that time, which in general is kind to all painting, will be kind also to ours. But a rapid journey through the rooms of any museum that houses our immediate predecessors will quickly undeceive that hope. I was shown the other day what I was told was Whistler's palette. I believe it was. For all the colors on it (as are the colors today in so many of his pictures), were quite black.

Time is not the only thing that is likely to be unkind to our pictures. Collectors and museums are frequently unkind as well, and painters are often distressed by a persistent and dangerous misconception in the popular mind as to what the nature of a picture actually is.

People who are not painters always think of pictures as ideas — as things that have their existence in the mind. Consequently, they treat them rough. Ideas can take rough treatment. A check for a hundred dollars is an idea. It is the symbol for an act — the act of passing over to someone else one hundred silver dollars (which are themselves symbols just as well). And no matter how much the check is rumpled or dirtied or injured or torn, its value as a symbol is not changed in the slightest as long as it exists at all. But a picture is not a symbol (although it too may be exchanged for money). And crumpling it or dirtying it or punching holes in it hurts it a great deal. Pictures are incredibly fragile; considering the tremendous punishment they receive, they are also incredibly sturdy. For years I have tried to show my mother that when pictures are stacked against a wall and the corner of one leans against the face of another, that corner will leave a dent that is very difficult to remove. She is a very good housekeeper. But that she will never learn. For she thinks of pictures as art. Janitors in museums are always sticking screwdrivers through masterpieces. People will hang pictures over radiators where their priming can be fortified by steam and their colors embellished by a generous deposit of soot. They will clean them with laundry soap or gasoline or ammonia, or send them to the local photographer's to be retouched. And then they are surprised at their pictures' appearance. Or perhaps they do not even notice. For most people do not see anything anyway.

There is a rule of behavior that is probably not in Emily Post, but should be observed by anyone who owns a picture. It is this: if your picture is dirty or has a hole in it or has mildewed or needs varnishing or is cracking or peeling or has suffered any one of the thousand accidents that can befall a picture, tell the painter himself and ask him what to do. Do not address yourself to any painter but the one who painted your picture, or he — and how right he is — will never forgive you. If the painter is dead or cannot be reached, find a competent restorer — not the local photographer or frame maker or decorator or school teacher who just loves art, but a real picture restorer who has a shop and equipment and prices (you can get his name from the nearest museum; they always have one) — and ask him what to do.

Of course, if pictures are not too dirty, they can be cleaned with potato juice or mild acetic acid. But I would not advise you to do it yourself. You will not know which to use, and you may easily damage a fragile ground. Never use soap and water on a picture; the soap is too hard to remove from the cracks of the paint and will do a lot of damage. Never use turpentine; it may dissolve your picture. Never use alcohol; you will find yourself faced with a bare canvas. Never oil your

picture with linseed oil; in six months it may turn
dark brown. Send your picture to a competent
restorer.

I have seen, in a local framer's, a small sixteenth-
century Flemish *Christ and the Doctors* painted
in tempera on a panel, which some GI had liberated; it was being further liberated by the framer,
who was daubing the injured spots with oil paint.
I am sure that the GI's mother for whom the
picture was intended would not have known the
difference. Nevertheless, the picture properly
taken care of would have had a certain money
value.

Some time ago I was asked to restore what the
owner called "two ancestral portraits." They were
charming pictures, probably painted in Vienna in
the forties or fifties, all very smooth and detailed,
each pearl in place. They were in a frightful state.
The glue that had held the painting ground to
the web of the canvas was completely gone. The
paint film had curled up in ribbons that looked
like curlicues of celluloid. To restore them would
have been an extraordinarily difficult job. I could
not undertake it. I told the owner to go to a restorer. Later I saw the pictures in a local jewelry
shop. The pictures were completely ruined; the
jeweler had restored them. Proud of his work, he
said: "These pictures were done in a very rare
technique. They were painted on paper." He had
mistaken the curled-up painting ground for dry-
rotten paper.

A proper restorer would have "relined" the ailing portraits, and if he knew his trade, no one could have guessed afterward that the pictures had ever been injured at all. The restorer would have taken the pictures off their stretchers, dampened or done something to the ribbons of paint film to make them lie flat, pasted sheet after sheet of tissue paper onto the surface of the picture until he had a strong enough support, turned the pictures over on their faces, separated the original canvas from the paint film — which the layers of tissue paper now hold firm — by moistening and pulling the canvas or by sandpapering it off, replaced the old canvas by a new and good one, which he would have glued on and ironed smooth with a warm flatiron, washed off the tissue paper, removed the old varnish, nailed the pictures back to their stretchers, mended the injured places by replacing the spots of missing ground and repainting them with tempera paint, which does not change color with age. And finally, the restorer would have revarnished the pictures, and they would have been as good as new. But as you can see, it is a complicated job and needs a patient and a skillful hand.

Restorers can do incredible things. They can even remove a fresco from the plaster of one wall and put it up on another. I once saw a Ghirlandajo painted on a wooden panel as big as a bed. The panel had warped and cracked, and the picture, face down on the restorer's workbench, was being transferred to another panel. The warped panel had been sawed and planed and sandpapered off. The plaster ground on which the picture was painted had been removed. And the back of the paint film itself was visible, with the first thin drawing lines in brown that the painter had put down when he began his picture.

In the early twenties an American collector bought in Europe for a very large sum a small Bellini, which he packed in a metal box, insured, and sent home. During the voyage fire broke out in the hold of the ship. The fire was extinguished but water got in the metal box and the Bellini was stewed. The insurance company paid, took the picture, box and all, and deposited it in a vacant room at their offices. The steam had destroyed the glue of the plaster ground the Bellini was painted on; the entire picture lay loose on the panel, one enormous blister. When an inquisitive office boy picked up the box to inspect it and let it slip, the whole mess slid to the floor and lay there in crumbs and dust of art. A museum bought the fragments. Its restorer locked himself in the vacant room, glued each small bit of picture to a piece of gauze — like Psyche sorting out the millet grains in the service of Love — fitted them together like a jigsaw puzzle on another panel, and painted in matching tones the few remaining gaps that were necessarily left. The picture can be seen today, and, except for the small missing spaces, which, if the museum had wished, the restorer could have easily concealed, no one could possibly imagine that anything had ever happened to it.

The restorer's great trick is the removal of overpainting. Oil paint takes a long time to dry; in fact, it is never completely dry. Overpainting put on a dry picture is never as hard, even years afterward, as the earlier paint. And the restorer can remove it by the use of differential solvents. That frequently has to be done. For a hat in a picture will have gone out of style, and somebody will have got a local artist to paint on a more fashionable one, or to touch up Great-aunt Elsie's face so she won't look so ugly. Often, instead of cleaning a picture, someone who is handy at things like that will have freshened it up with a new coat of paint till it is as good as new.

Some time ago the administrators of an Eastern museum bought a small daub that they claimed was a Botticelli. Documents, they said, proved it authentic. It was late Botticelli, perhaps done after he had been reformed by Savonarola and had thrown all his pictures in the fire. Probably his conversion had also made him forget how to paint. Everybody in the museum who had any actual sense about painting rejoiced — the authorities had at last put their foot in it; the picture was undeniably a daub — until it was sent to the restorer's for cleaning. He removed the overpainting and revealed a jewel of a Botticelli in perfect condition.

As an example of restoration in reverse, a restorer told me of a lady who came to him with a portrait of a Civil War ancestor wearing a long stringy beard. "I want you," she said, "to trim off some of the beard and show his necktie. You know I have always been a great admirer of General Lee."

There is also that old chestnut about the American who bought a Rembrandt in Europe, and to avoid the customs, the property tax, or something of the sort, had an impressionist landscape — that will give you an idea of the age of the joke — painted on it before he shipped it home. Once home, he sent it to a restorer to have the impressionist picture removed. Shortly afterward he received a letter from the restorer who wrote: "Dear Sir: We have removed the landscape and the Rembrandt and come to a portrait of George the Third. Shall we go farther?" The joke is not very funny because that is just what restorers do.

They can also exaggerate. There are fashions in restorations as in anything else. If clean pictures are in fashion, restorers will remove, with the varnish, all the painter's finishing touches and leave the picture distressingly naked. And if antique-looking pictures are in demand, they have been known to mix a little bitumen in their final varnish. A friend of mine claims to have seen one of them in a museum standing before a small Sienese Madonna with a brush and a pot of paint in his hands. The walls of the gallery had evidently been painted blue to match the background of the picture. But the color had not come out right. So

the restorer was doing the easier thing. He was repainting the background of the picture to go with
the walls of the room.

From all this one can understand why painters
are a little uneasy when they send their pictures to
exhibitions, and always examine them carefully
for possible injuries on their return, and why they
are upset when they find their pictures hung over
a radiator in a client's house, and why they peer
uneasily into the corners of their early works
searching for color changes or cracks. For the signs
of decay in his picture are the germs of mortality
of the painter's fame. But however unhappy the
bad state of a picture may render the painter, it is
nothing compared with the unhappiness he experiences when he is faced with the problem of
frames. And although frames are not actually
part of the painter's tools, I will nevertheless
speak of them here, for they are a necessary part
of the mechanism for turning painting into art —
a process that fascinates the painter as much, and
that he understands as little, as the problem of
framing itself.

If painting nowadays were done like painting
in the past, if the whole approach to making pictures had not been changed by the impressionists,
framing, though it would still be difficult and expensive, would not be the nightmare it is today to
the painter, the picture buyer, and everybody else.
The painter, the framer, and the collector, all go

off into a panic of indecision when the word "frame" is pronounced. For the methods of composition and painting have completely changed, and the solution of the framing problem, which worked so well for the older painting, will not work at all for the paintings of the present day. Modern pictures will not take gold frames.

The gold frame is a tradition handed down from the time when the primary purpose of a small picture was to decorate chests and altarpieces and other gilded furniture with scenes from legends and from the lives of the saints, and when the small picture was actually painted in tempera on a gold background. The gold frame is an inheritance from the gold ornamentation of the furniture itself. Gold leaf has always been laid on a brick-red ground. That is the color of the Armenian bole — a sort of red clay — that was put on the plaster of the panels and carvings and that glued the gold leaf down and enabled it to be burnished. Later, to assure the unity of the painting and the customary gold frame, pictures were commonly painted on a brick-red ground almost the same color as the bole. In most of these pictures the general tone of the background is dark. Against the dark the light areas form the accents and the pattern of the picture. For the painter has been careful to see that nothing of any importance, no accented light areas, will come against the gold of the frame. The picture has been planned to be a pattern of bright objects surrounded by dark, which in turn is surrounded by the bright frame. In framing, the only things to be watched are that the size of the detail of the frame matches the size of the detail in the picture, that the width and depth of the frame are not so great that the picture looks small and crowded, or so little that the frame looks meager and poor, and that the workmanship of the frame is carefully enough done and expensive enough looking to accord with the market value of the picture.

Pictures painted during the last eighty years will not accept so simple a choice. To obtain greater luminosity, painters since the impressionists have painted on white grounds. The darks, and not the lights, now form the accents and the pattern of the picture. Influenced, with or without his conscious knowledge, by the Japanese print and with the purpose of making his picture equally interesting all over, the painter will bring his design up to the very edge of his canvas. A gold frame will no longer do. The tone of the picture is no longer golden or yellow, and swears at a gold enclosure. The dark accents are likely to bleed over into the frame. A white frame, matching the white ground, is more becoming to a modern picture. But a white frame seldom goes with the decoration of a room and always looks inexpensive, which, of all things, is least desired by everybody. The gold frame, at least, had the natural advantage of always looking costly. The problem faced by the present-day framer is to make a frame look rich and yet not be gold. It is very difficult. The best solution is — like the old tweed coat, threadbare but from a good tailor — a carved and gilded frame from which the gilding has been removed. But for a frame to look properly rich, it must be a carved frame and not a plaster one. An old coat which was not well made in the beginning has no chic. But even a *décapé* frame of this sort will not isolate the modern picture enough; the picture is still likely to bleed over into the frame. So to isolate it still more a neutral band — a "marie louise" — of painted wood or natural linen is generally inserted between the picture and the frame. With a band of this sort even a gold frame, if suitably dulled down, can sometimes be used.

The primary purpose of framing is to concentrate the spectator's attention on the picture, to limit the picture, and isolate it on the wall. The frame should not attract attention to itself. It should not be too different in style from the other furnishings of the room, should be as carefully made as the oil surface of the picture itself, and should look as rich and sumptuous as the social standing and the market value of the picture will allow.

As a matter of fact, this last is precisely the second and equally important function of a frame — to define a picture's social standing and market value. And, just as a man can be well dressed in any number of ways — in overalls, pajamas, slacks, tweeds, tails, or nothing at all — and how he is dressed depends on what he is going to do and in what company he is going to do it, so a picture can be well framed in any number of ways depending on what it is expected to do and where it is going to hang. But the living painter has no idea of his picture's eventual intellectual tone or what its social tone will eventually be, where it will hang, how much it will be worth, and what company it is going to keep. All he knows is that he painted as well as he could something that interested him. And that is no help to him at all.

Consequently, framing is always a headache to the painter. Frames are not only difficult to choose, they are awkward to store as well, and owning them commits the painter to making pictures in sizes he already has frames for. And for some reason or other — perhaps the natural perversity of the human mind — when a painter paints a picture especially for a frame he already has, the frame never suits the picture he intended for it. So painters seldom own frames if they can help it, and when they need a frame, many painters avoid the difficulty of an empty guess and an expensive decision by putting around the picture strips of black or white painted wood, which serve the primary purpose of framing by concentrating the spectator's attention and isolating the picture from the wall, but which are easily disposed of, and which do not compromise the picture by involv-

ing it in any social tone or style of decoration.
That is all well enough as far as it goes. But then
the painter expects that when the picture is sold,
the buyer will get his own frame to suit his own
interior — a thing which, unfortunately, no buyer
is either capable of doing or willing to attempt.

So, in search of expert advice, the painter seeks
out the specialist in the definition of social tone,
the interior decorator. But there he is barking up
the wrong tree. For the decorator is a specialist in
defining the social standing, not of the pictures of
a living painter, but of his own client. And that
the decorator must do, not with such equivocal
material as our painter's pictures, but with things
whose social position is already secure. Unable
to get help from the decorator, the painter goes to
the nearest picture framer and spends hours of
agony and indecision trying out inadequate frames
and idiotic ideas. He knows that he is going to
choose wrong anyway. So he refuses to spend
enough money and the frame comes out looking,
along with its other faults, cheap. He is never
satisfied, and feels guilty about framing as something he should know all about, but that is really
out of his control. For he knows that no one will
know how to frame his pictures until they are
completely acceptable as art, until their social and
intellectual tone is firmly established and he himself is dead. So that although he thinks he should
be, he is not capable of being interested in framing
at all.

Nevertheless, in spite of this inadequacy in front of his own work, the painter is a perfectly good judge of those qualities that will enable a painting possessing them to be eventually converted into art, and consequently into money. And as I have already told the reader at the beginning of this chapter how to tell a good painter, now I will disclose to him another and — because it may mean money in his pocket — even more valuable secret: how to know what picture to buy. Here it is:

Put a painter in front of a picture and ask him.

The painter is, I assure you, the only one in the world who knows anything about painting. If you can get him to talk about a picture, you will probably have to discount his natural malice toward a rival — which is tremendous — or get behind his reluctant politeness, his hesitancy in saying something disobliging about a fellow artist. But then you will find out what he knows. And he does know, for he has been trained to see. And what he sees today, other people will see tomorrow. But, mind you, it must be an opinion about a picture he has really seen, preferably about one he is actually looking at. At a distance he will dislike too much the abstract idea of another painter, both his work and his subject matter. Looking at the picture will clear his mind. He will see the work itself without being confused by its style, fashionableness, or subject matter, and he will tell you its actual qualities.

Degas was notoriously the most difficult, the

most malicious man in all Paris. But Vollard, the picture dealer, got on to Cézanne, and a considerable fortune, because Degas, when asked, said to him: "That fellow Cézanne is the best of us all."

CHAPTER VI

BEAUTY

"I saw a picture just like that in the five-and-ten. But it had a frame."

(VERMONT FARMER)

WHEN I was a beginner learning to paint, I was more than a little bothered because I seemed to have very little to do with beauty. I soon found, however, much more interesting things than that to worry about, and quickly discovered that, of all the possible subjects of painting, beauty is the least satisfactory. As a subject for painting, beauty is either too disturbing to the peace of mind or too trite. For beauty is an emotion, and it is provoked by two things and by two things alone: by something we want to possess or by memories of art. A person we can imagine ourselves in love with, or in bed with, is beautiful; a sunset is beautiful when it reminds us of a picture we have seen. Neither of these states of mind leads to original work. So, the painter painting beauty is either seeing it at second hand and copying a picture that has already been painted by someone else, or he is painting, not what he sees, but the emotions the thing he is seeing arouses in him. And unless he can find in the thing he is painting another quality than beauty to point his attention, his subject will dazzle him and he will go blind.

Interest is that other quality. Anything that is interesting to look at can be painted. But beauty is not interesting to look at; it is a fascination, a cause of bewilderment. It cannot be used; it is itself the aggressor. It does not fix the attention; on the contrary, it destroys the attention by turning the spectator's interest from the thing he is looking at to the feelings the thing is causing within him. It is an enchantment, a magic spell. It enchants the beholder, bemuses him. He cannot see clearly, and if he is a painter, he cannot paint. And the painter who is painting beauty is in a bad way unless he is using the word "beauty" as the generic name for his subject matter. In that case he is merely being pretentious and is not painting beauty at all, but only the things that he and others have found interesting to look at. Children, I am sure, are all beautiful. But the painter who actually finds them so will have a mighty hard time with the little bastards.

So that proposition number one of this æsthetic is: beauty is not a fit subject for painting. Proposition number two is just as rude: a beautiful picture is a dead picture.

Pictures, when they are fresh painted, are not beautiful. They can not even be sold. People will always buy a painter's older pictures in preference

to the ones he has just finished, even though the
new ones are better painted and will themselves
in a few years sell like hot cakes. A contemporary
picture is not beautiful. It may be interesting. It
may attract the eye often and hold it long. It may
be arresting, disturbing, amazing, revealing. It
may show you things you never saw before. But
it cannot be beautiful. Nor will it be until the
painter is dead and cannot do it any more, until
fashion has changed and people have different
things on their minds and the picture has lost its
disturbing actuality, until no one remembers what
the picture was all about and all that remains
within its frame are the formal perfection of its
proportions and its existence in the nostalgia of
the more nearly perfect world of an untroubled
past — until the picture is thoroughly and completely dead.

This is why:

Fashion and the need for change are not a trivial joke or a domestic silliness. We are likely to
think of fashion as silly and unnecessary because
what comes to our mind is yesterday's ugly and
unnecessary hat and how silly were all the ladies
who wanted it — forgetting that yesterday the hat
may have been funny, but that it was neither ugly
nor unnecessary, and that tomorrow it will be
charming. Fashion is neither silly nor unnecessary.
It is one of the major forces of the world, and has
to do with how everybody, everywhere, at the
same time, unreasonably and quite spontaneously,

finds a new and different thing interesting to look at, and envisages this new thing under a new set of proportions — how everybody finds the new set of proportions quite normal, in fact forgets that any other set of proportions can exist, and discovers that the things they have just stopped being interested in and the proportions they have just stopped using have become unutterably stupid and ugly.

This new set of proportions is fashion itself, its bones and flesh and sinews. What fashion operates on, its subject matter, so to speak, is the new thing that everybody is looking at at that moment: what people have on their minds, how they envisage the world, and what disguise they wish to assume to make themselves feel more at home in it.

What everybody has on his mind depends on the philosophical and scientific discoveries of his times. One of the major achievements of the Greeks was their mathematics. They brought the methods of geometry to such perfection that it was not until Descartes, some eighteen centuries later, that any addition was made to their treatment of the conic sections. These, the circle, elipse, parabola, and hyperbola, together with the Archimedean spiral, were their triumphs. So, it can surprise no one that Greek temples, instead of being in straight lines and cylindrical columns, are gently varied and twisted to follow these subtle curves. Baroque architecture embodied the intricate volutes and curves-in-three-dimensions that the new Cartesian analysis had discovered. The nineteenth century had the style of the Eiffel Tower, its department stores, and splendid railway terminals, because its engineers had found the use of structural iron and steel. And because of our airplanes and our wind tunnels, we have our streamlined beds and toilet seats. In every case the new discoveries are on everybody's mind, and everything that everybody does, even in the most unrelated fields, is a tribute to the new ideas.[1]

Clothes are, of course, most obviously and amusingly subject to fashion. Here the subject matter is very apparent. Fashion describes what people suppose is their relation to the world and how they wish to look and feel.

Clothes can be designed for concealment or for high visibility. Ecclesiastical costume is designed for concealment. Here it is the ceremony that is important, not the performer. The priest is turned by his vestment — waistless and shapeless — into an anonymous unit for celebrating the glory of God. The alb and the cope are not tailored; the miter and stole fit the office, not the man. For it is the ceremony that must be seen. And the gestures of the officiant at Mass do not have to carry any distance at all — only far enough to reach the throne of God.

[1] Even supernatural beings are subject to this rule. Before the beginning of our century, witches were accustomed to ride their broomsticks to Sabbath with the head of the broom, like a horse's head, in front. Today they assume the more efficient air-flow position.

On the other hand, in an epoch when the great personages of the world must appear before the world as on a stage, whatever they do in public must be completely visible both to the pit and the gallery. So that in all times of court and pomp and ceremony, when the individual human being is the star and actor, the human body is, by fashion, articulated like an insect's, divided into limbs, head, abdomen, and thorax, so that each of its attitudes can be seen from far off. In man, the arms and legs are separated from the body by clothing them so tightly that their extension is revealed, and by accenting with huge puffs the point where they join the trunk — or by covering the limbs loosely up to the shoulder and the crotch, where the garment is pulled tight to make more apparent all the articulations. The head is isolated from the shoulders by a ruff, or the length of neck is emphasized by an imposing headdress. The body is divided in two by a girdle or a corset or a false rump. Frequently the great cape is worn, which makes its wearer seem larger than life and underlines his gestures. The woman's dress has a narrow waist and a huge skirt. Everything is designed to be seen from far away. For the pose of the head and the positions of the body must indicate the grandeur and the dignity that the perhaps invisible severity of the visage cannot convey.

The costume of the ballet is in this tradition. The ballerina's tutu, the little puffs on her shoulders, her hair on the top of her head, and her legs in simple tights, turn the human body into a mathematical instrument for making the measurement of space visible from a distance, a semaphore for transmitting to the farthest spectator messages of position and sentiment. And so successfully does it work that the accomplished dancer never has to smile.

The costumes of the courts of Louis XIV and Louis XV were intended for public show and designed for high visibility. But in the more intimate court of Louis XVI, great receptions went out of style. The most envied gatherings were those *en petit comité*. So the hair of the ladies was allowed to fall on the shoulders, covering the joinings of the neck, and the waist was concealed by a wrap resembling the domestic dressing gown. For the ladies were supposed to be seen from near by. But on the other hand think of Henry VIII of England, and of Elizabeth, dressed like a king and queen of chess, both visible from afar and royal indeed.

At Monticello, the house Jefferson built for himself in Virginia, I was taken upstairs in the company of two Southern ladies. The stairs were dark and narrow, I suppose because Jefferson, as a good Democrat, disapproved of the pompous *escalier d'honneur,* which in a French house of any pretension was designed for the sort of courtly display of clothes and deportment of which I have been speaking. My two ladies were much astonished. "How," they said, "did the women get up and down these narrow stairs in their great big skirts?" They had forgotten that Monticello was built at the time of the "Greek" and "Republican" *Directoire,* when a fashionable lady's dress was so skimpy that everything she wore could be passed through her wedding ring. They were remembering only the ample skirts worn by the mistresses of Louis XV and by the wife of Napoleon III. So that by confusing the styles of the two times and forgetting the century that came between, they were able to attribute an extreme and almost Chinese antiquity to our own Civil War. I, in my turn, was reminded that no Southern Cotton Ball can be complete without the ladies in their antebellum gowns, copied from the fashion plates of 1760, an error of only a hundred years.

I think that the people of the eighteenth century must have liked to feel important. Eighteenth-century chairs and tables and ceiling were low, and though the rooms were not always small, they were usually so light in proportion and in such light, clear colors that their delicacy made people in them seem very large. People of the eighteenth century must also have enjoyed feeling old and wise. For the powdered hair and the costume that hid all but the man's calf and the woman's bosom, were in no way becoming to youth, flattered age, and disguised them both in an ageless permanence. In middle Victorian times people obviously pretended to a great personal reticence, for the proportions of their rooms were so heavy, their furniture so massive, and the patterns of their fabrics and wall papers so assertive that anyone placed among them almost disappeared, as did their private life, from public view. The mid-Victorian gentleman's dress was black — partly, in the dark and mephitic city air, to protect the garment from stain, partly to conceal the man. The gilt and mirrors of Louis XIV boasted that his was the greatest court of Europe, for no amount of dirt or handling or misuse by courtiers could possibly obscure their splendor. We, with our recent enthusiasm for white, can only be boasting of our affluence. For in a soot-colored world nothing can be kept white without an infinite attendance of servants — the most expensive thing of modern times. Nothing can better indicate the wealth of its tenant than the spotless white of a Le Corbusier flat.

Fashion uses costume to define social position as well. The upper classes do not labor. The well-dressed man must not be thought able to demean himself by work. Consequently, the formal costume of all times, even when hand-to-hand fighting is the chief sport of nobles, is designed to hinder the free movements of the body. Only the duelist and billiard player — both indisputably upper class — may remove their coats. I have even been tempted to believe that the knights of the Middle Ages, in the elaborate and practically immovable armor we now see in museums, took no part in fighting at all and made only a formal appearance on the field, that the battles were fought by their squires and soldiers in lighter equipment, and that the heavy armor was of purely honorific use, intended to protect its wearer, not from the enemies' lances, but from the imputation that he himself could engage in actual combat.

I am informed, however, that the armor of the museums is not battle armor at all, but is a very carefully preserved and decorative panoply — the white tie of the Middle Ages — intended not to be worn in battle, but at parties and jousts. The working armor of the time, just as the working clothes of all time, has long ago disappeared, worn out with use, its fragments used up as patches and rivets and hand-me-down pants for Junior when he became old enough himself to go out and fight the paynim.

Fashion may also, by means of clothes, describe what people would like to be but cannot be, what disguise they would like to assume. It provides, by means of a masquerade, the symbol of the attainment of an unattainable desire.

The easiest example of this is, of course, the codpiece of the sixteenth century. That carapace and brooch for the lower belly, inflated and stiffened with whalebone and bombast, claimed for its wearer an excessive and permanent virility and denied that the flesh is weak. Or the fashion of the shaved face, which in all times, save when the patriarch is ruler of the tribe and family and consequently is envied and emulated, denies that youth

can pass. The Roman gentleman carried this artificial youth to such an excess that as a preparation
and as a costume for love, he epilated his whole
body.

We all remember the fashions after the first
World War. I imagine people were tired of responsibility and wanted to get back to childhood.
So they dressed themselves up. The men put on
the costume of a fourteen-year-old schoolboy —
golf pants like the knickers of their childhood,
and short, tight coats like little Eton jackets. The
ladies dressed themselves up like little girls, in a
low waistline, short skirts, and bobbed hair, and
carried themselves so that they would appear to
have no breasts at all. Both disguises were almost
sexless, a brother-and-sister act. Ever since the ending of that war the dress designers tried to change
the styles and bring back the long skirt. No Paris
fashion show was complete without one. The
cloth manufacturers wanted the long skirt back
because it would take more goods; the dress designers wanted it because they were tired of Chanel. But the public would not have it. Then in
1929 the long skirt came in — snap — just like
that. Perhaps it was on account of the stock-market
crash and the desire for a different sort of world.
Perhaps it was because the girls were tired of being only companions to the men and wanted to
feel again that they were dangerous and mysterious and Mata Haraish. It may have been simply
that people had played long enough at being chil-

dren and wanted to be grown-up. All of a sudden
public drunkenness, which every one had found
so amusing before, was no longer fun. Overnight
the long skirt came back (it took the girls some
time to learn to walk in them) and overnight the
golf pants disappeared. No one has ever worn
them since, even for golf. The brother-and-sister
act was over. For a while people were again men
and women.

The zoot suit of recent years was, I think, another infantilism. The too-large pants, the too-
long coat, the enormous hat, the drooping watch
chain, were a wearing of Papa's clothes, and went
along with dances that recalled the singing games
of children in their figures and in the expressions
on the faces of their dancers. The zoot suit was
most popular with our two most oppressed popu-
lations, the colored people and the Spanish-speak-
ing people of the Southwest. The unhappy sons
and daughters of the depression had taken it as
their traveling costume and were going back to
childhood.

Certain standard costumes for certain professions are certainly by way of being disguises. The
American banker would not think of dressing
himself in anything but a Brooks Brothers suit or
its equivalent. That combination of discreet material and sexless cutting is designed to make him
look exactly the opposite of the traditional card-
sharp — which he probably is. I suppose Parisian
journalists, a venal and unhappy race, still dress

in wide black hats and Windsor ties, disguising themselves in the habit worn in other years, as a badge of free love and socialism, by free and happy artists. Professors, since they do not live the country life, even in the country-club colleges, dress themselves in tweeds. A tweed coat and flannel trousers (supposed, I imagine, to represent something brought back from an undergraduate reading party in Scotland) have for a number of years replaced the scholar's gown as a symbol of the academic life. In England at the present moment, corduroy is scarce and difficult to obtain. To get it one must have an agriculturer's ration card, which is not possible except for the farmer or the gentleman farming his own estate. Consequently, no English artist of today dares appear in London society unless he is dressed in the corduroys of the landed proprietor. No producer or director of Hollywood could possibly be seen in public in anything but a sport coat — sport being perhaps the one thing he does not do. There is a new fashion coming from there, and much affected by the bourgeoisie of the place: an enormous jacket, obviously designed for the carrying of concealed weapons — the gangster influence.

Fashion, as what disguise one wants to assume, is also apparent in architecture. The reasonable eighteenth-century gentleman, tired of his reasonableness, sought a change in the ruder, fiercer Gothic and in a taste for ruins. There was a man in France who blew his house up with gunpowder and built another across the valley whence he could contemplate his ruins. There are ruins in England that have been blown up for the same picturesque purpose two and three times. There are Roman ruins in Paris — and very pretty they are, too — built in the eighteenth century. Since modern governments want to appear as governmental as possible and since Rome is obviously, as any reader of Plutarch knows, the best governmental model, modern government and administration buildings always disguise themselves as the Roman Forum — not yet in ruins. Colleges, if they have a church affiliation, dress themselves up in a happy mingling of collegiate and ecclesiastical Gothic. If they are purely secular they will turn to the Georgian model so compactly reiterated by Harvard, and will repeat themselves on every countryside in brick and white-painted wooden cornice, until one is sure that the Red Coats are coming and Paul Revere will soon ride by. Movie palaces have a tendency to affect the Moorish style, on the principle that, after all, the most satisfactory entertainment is that of the harem.

Nevertheless, I do not believe that any fashion or disguise will be accepted by everybody, unless everybody really wants it. I do not think that a fashion can be successfully imposed from above. And I am led to believe that the bug-shaped automobile, the streamlined icebox and hearse (it is pretty in French: *le corbillard aérodynamique*) are fashions popular not with the public, but with the manufacturers, who would like to feel as advanced in their designs as they are conservative in their politics. For when the jeep appeared, not streamlined at all but practically designed for its purpose, all the world took it to its bosom with a loud whoop.

But all this — these evidences of what a time has on its mind and these disguises people assume — is only the subject matter of fashion, not fashion itself. Fashion itself is this new set of proportions that is visible and seems right to its time. And this is the mystery: not that the thing people are looking at should change or that they should tire of the old and become interested in something new, but that the shape in which they see the new thing changes as well and even more astonishingly. The new set of proportions is not imposed by any one authority. Its choice seems to follow no known rule or pattern. It just happens. Every ten years or so proportions change and everything that is built or done during the period is trade-marked with the same set of proportions. The ante-bellum gown of Southern society has not the proportions of 1860, but of Hollywood today. The collegiate Gothic of Duke University resembles only faintly its possible model, the church at Brou. The Harvard Business School, erected in the twenties, has completely different proportions from its model — Holden chapel, built by the same college in the eighteenth century. It even has different proportions from the former freshman dormitories, built after the identical model only thirty years ago. Examine the suburban domestic architecture built in this country during the last ten years. Whether rich or poor, in brick, stone, or wood, it is all exactly alike: the same lack of cornice, the same series of interlocking rectangular parallelepipeds surmounted by the same flattened isosceles prisms, and all of exactly the same shape and proportion — a Rooseveltian style.

(The lack of cornice is characteristic of American architecture. It has to do, I suppose, with our very clear light. In France and England, where the light is softer, cornices grow to the enormous weight necessary in that foggy light to cast a shadow and make an accent. Farther south in Europe where the sun is brighter, houses are more likely to adopt the shape of simple boxes. Here in America a hairline on a wall will cast a sufficient shadow. The climate of New York in recent years seems to be changing; with its more numerous factories its air is becoming increasingly smoky. If this continues our new buildings will doubtless be ornamented with heavier detail.)

We built ourselves an American Embassy in Paris on the Place de la Concorde, copying a seventeenth-century hotel across the square. The architect had his model under his nose. With the help of a foot rule, a pair of dividers and a good ladder he could measure everything. Undoubtedly he did. Nevertheless when the Embassy was finished it turned out a modern American building, nothing at all like the model. Because it was impossible for the architect to copy the seventeenth-century building without correcting its proportions by the only set of proportions anybody is ever able to employ — the proportions of his time.

And this is a general truth. Whenever an epoch imitates a past style, it does so in its own characteristic proportions. A copyist, for example, will be able to make a forgery of an old master that will pass unsuspected in his own time. To a later time the fraud will appear astonishingly undeceiving. Because the forger will have been able to copy only the qualities of his model that were visible to his own time, and only in the proportions that his own time was accustomed to use. These are neither the qualities and proportions the old master actually possesses nor the qualities and proportions that a later time will attribute to it.

Since Classical and Gothic times every epoch has had artists who imitated as closely as they could the Classical and the Gothic styles. There was even in ancient Rome a pre-Phidian school of sculpture. Michelangelo, Canova, Rodin, Maillol, and our own Paul Manship all followed what they considered to be the classical Greek style. Nevertheless their work is completely unalike. For each one worked in the style of his own time. Viollet-le-Duc, the great nineteenth-century Gothic architect and restorer, rebuilt stone by stone the walled town of Carcassonne, and left it the most perfect monument, not of the medieval, but of his own age, looking to our present-day eyes more like the drawings of his contemporary, Victor Hugo, than like any of the authentic medieval monuments we are familiar with. Viollet-le-Duc restored, as well, the church of Notre Dame of Paris, and designed and placed upon its towers its celebrated gargoyles. Today these gargoyles look more like the devils that decorate an "infernal style" Montmartre night club than like any of the devils who might have actually inhabited France in the thirteenth century. Ralph Adams Cram, the American ecclesiastical architect, built an American church in Paris some years ago. In an interview to the newspapers he was quoted as saying that in his opinion the Gothic was the most beautiful of all architectural styles and that the French was the most beautiful of all the Gothics; but that in France unfortunately there was no perfect example of the French Gothic style. So he had built them one. His building came out, indeed, a Gothic church, but scarcely in the French style. It is rather, as is natural enough, in our own American high-church Episcopalian tradition and has, I understand, even a drinking fountain. (Morris Gest once rebuilt the interior of New York's Century Theater in the Gothic style for the presentation of a devotional play, and disguised the necessary drinking fountains as baptismal fonts.) The stained-glass windows of Notre Dame of Paris, destroyed during the French Revolution and restored by Viollet-le-Duc, now resemble less his models in Chartres, than do to our contemporary eyes the paintings of Rouault, who, I suppose, has gone to the same source for his style and subject. But no one can say that either the windows of Notre Dame or the paintings of Rouault are not both complete works and monuments characteristic of their times.

So that no matter what we paint or build, with what subject matter or in what imagined style, we work in the style of today. What we do now is not beautiful, it is what we are able to see, it is what is capable of holding the attention. And the criterion of its excellence is not that it looks beautiful, but that it looks right. It is what we are able to understand. For however much we may admire the past, we can understand only the present. I recently heard a high-school orchestra perform an easy classical concert ending up with a modern piece. Their Beethoven was not good. The students were beginners and had not yet learned a proper way of interpreting the Romantic composers, of transposing them to the present. But when they came to Copland the students went to town. There no training in interpretation was necessary. That music they understood without preparation: it was of their time.

The present-day proportions are like the lenses of the eye. We see through them, we do not see the proportions themselves. But once tomorrow is come and the new proportions have become the

normal ones, yesterday's proportions are no longer
the framework of our seeing and they become
themselves visible as an outlandish and absurd
convention. Nor are the works executed under
their canons any longer part of our time. We no
longer completely understand them, no longer
know what they were about. Our attention becomes fixed on their strange proportions, which
we find first strange and ugly and then strange
and beautiful. For, as Bacon said, there is no excellent beauty that hath not some strangeness in
the proportion.

An object that has remained too long in the
limbo of ugliness, in that blind spot which follows
our passage through time, may often be brought
out of it and made visible by changing its color or
its texture. The shock of seeing an accustomed object in a new skin will enable the eye to perceive
that it has form and proportion and is perhaps
well made. The nineteenth century painted all
eighteenth-century furniture Trianon gray and
was in that way able to see it. There was a time
when all Gothic was varnished dark brown, and
when the brown of Mission furniture became the
symbol for the intellectual life. We painted Victorian furniture white and called it "Federal."
Now it has become visible again and we can have
it in any color, even its own, and call it by its
right name. It is perhaps because the violin has always been in use and has always been regarded as
an instrument of music and not as an objet d'art

that it, alone of all baroque sculpture, has never had to suffer a change of color or of surface to make it acceptable to a later world. For everything else does. Even pictures are resurfaced. Titians are skinned. Rembrandts are drowned in an aquarium of varnish. Modern pictures are made visible by the proper frames and by the painter's death.

The painter, trained as he is to see, has perceived the new proportions a little before anybody else, and as long as he is alive he keeps a little ahead of the public's seeing. Though his early pictures have by this time become strange and possibly beautiful, his present ones are only interesting. Because the pictures he is painting now are pictures of things everybody knows about or will soon be knowing about, and are painted in the proportions everybody is using or will soon be using. Consequently, his present pictures are not beautiful or mysterious in any way. And they will in no way resemble art. That is what the cubist pictures were in our youth. They were not art but they were fun. Now they are art. Now they are what art is — the classified subject matter for academic discourse and the valuable property of 57th Street dealers — but they are somewhat duller.

While the painter is alive his work sells for one of two reasons: either because someone has a liking or a use for a particular subject and is employing the painter in his professional capacity to paint a picture of it for him, or it is because someone is speculating on the painter's death and sub-

sequent apotheosis. Either because the painter's
work pleases a client or because the painter's pictures may later become art. But once the painter
is dead he cannot disappoint or surprise any more.
All his work can be seen, the differences of quality become apparent, the bad pictures can be discarded, and the proper frames can be invented. As
I have already pointed out, though many frames
may be becoming to a picture, there is only one
that will properly define the social standing, the
intellectual position, and the market value of the
work. As these qualities are now visible, framing
is no longer a problem. The number of pictures is
now limited, the market price may be established
on the basis of quality and rarity, and the paintings become art — and are justly called beautiful.

Although beauty in art may have had its origin
in truth, for that is what the painter was looking
at when he was at work, the actual equivalence of
this beauty — which can only be measured in how
much anybody wants it and is willing to pay for
it — is market value.

Chapter VII

MONEY, MUSEUMS, AND MERCHANTS

"She was going to be an opera singer. But she got saved."

(EAST TENNESSEE LADY EVANGELIST)

PROFESSIONS can all be sorted into two broad classes, depending on whether they deal with objects or with abstract ideas. On one side are the engineer with his bridges, the mechanic with his tools, the painter with his paints and brushes, the doctor with his drugs and patients — all doing special things to particular objects, objects that can be seen, touched, handled, manipulated by the co-ordination of hand, mind, and eye. On the other side are the trades that have to do with the intangibles, things we know exist but cannot see, whose effects we can feel, whose presence is not in time and space, but in our own minds — the spiritual values. Such is the occupation of the lawyer, who deals with those strained abstractions of our deeds and desires that can be contained in words; of the press agent, who creates esteem out of the wind; of the theologian, the spiritual leader, the

newspaper man, the politician, who direct the cur-
rents of our trust. And with them goes the trade
that serves the most spiritual of all values, the
most abstract of all ideas, the entity that, because
it can be measured, we all assume automatically
and falsely to be with us here and now, as a material substance, in our pockets and in our banks,
whose absence and presence affect us more than
food or warmth or love itself, that has a life completely independent of our own but no existence
of any sort outside our own minds — the banker
and the money he counts.

Beauty in a work of art is also one of the spiritual values. For beauty is not a material attribute
of any picture. It exists only in the beholder's
mind. It is the measure of how desirable the work
of art is to one particular person. Consequently,
beauty can scarcely be said to be a universal scale.
A picture or a face may be impossibly attractive
to one person and to another may mean nothing
at all. Money value, on the other hand, is a measure that has a more general acceptance than beauty
and is more easily applied. For money value meas-
ures the number of people who find a particular
sort of thing beautiful against the number of that
sort of thing there is to be sold. The sentence "the
Rembrandt is beautiful" means that John Doe or
Allen Smith or Thomas Aquinas, or whoever said
it, wants the picture. The sentence "the Rembrandt is worth fifty thousand dollars" means that
the number of people who find the Rembrandt

beautiful divided by the number of Rembrandts on the market is equal to a monetary constant times fifty thousand:

$$n/m = 50,000 \; k$$

The picture merchant belongs on the side of the spiritual values. His job is the manipulation of my formula. For though the constant k is beyond his control — that being the occupation of the banker, the economist, the politician and the general staff — n and m, the number of people who admire the painting and the number of pictures there is to be sold can both be juggled with. A discreet use of the poets, the critics, and the literary world, a refined publicity campaign, and fictitious sales between merchants (where nothing but pictures changes hands, but prices get marked upon the books) will do wonders for n. And m can frequently be arranged by withdrawing pictures from the market, and even sometimes by a careful use of Solomon's sword.

You will notice that Rembrandt himself does not enter into my formula in any way. He has been paid off long ago. The market value of something that is now a work of art is always a resale value. And although this value does not in general diminish, as does the resale value of an automobile, which wears out with use, neither Rembrandt nor his heirs have any advantage from the subsequent sales of his works, except to the honor of his name.

Nevertheless it is Rembrandt himself in partic-

ular and the painter himself in general who make
this elaborate commerce possible. The dealer, however much he would like to, cannot create a demand. He can only make use of a demand that already exists, and the demand has as its origin the
painter himself. It is the painter, while he is yet
alive, who creates the nucleus for it, the next egg,
the small number of people who begin to want his
pictures. This is all the easier for him if he lives in
a world where people already have the habit of
picture buying. Then he will not have to waste
too much of his time persuading clients and can
spend more of his time painting pictures. If he is
using his eyes and is worth his salt, he will be
painting the world around him as he sees it at the
time in which he is painting — in the present, so
to speak. His friends who understand him and
the people with "flair" will start buying. Now,
flair is a very curious thing. It means an ability to
predict the present. And very useful it is to a picture merchant, who if he has it will be able to buy
cheap what he will later sell dear.

What I mean by "predicting the present" is
this: a painter in a painting center is painting
what is present there at that moment. That present travels from the center to the provinces. But it
takes a certain time to arrive because it travels by
the dissemination of the painter's works. Some va-
rieties of the present travel faster than others. It
took the cubists only about three years to cross the
Atlantic. It took Cézanne almost twenty. For

someone who is on the spot where the painting is being done, flair is easier to have. It only amounts to seeing (as the name would imply) what is under one's nose. But in the provinces, flair is more difficult to exercise. There it partakes of the nature of a supersensory perception — a thing that I am assured exists, but which is notoriously hard to turn to use in one's own daily living.

Nevertheless, whether in the center or in the province, whether a client collects his pictures or a merchant speculates in them, any sort of buying at all helps the painter. Nothing creates confidence in him and brings him sales as much as other sales. In fact, the only difference between the amateur painter and the professional painter is that the professional painter has sold one picture. That one sale becomes evident in all his work. The sale gives style to the picture that is sold and makes visible the style of his other works as well. There is no flattery to the painter as sincere as the act of buying a picture. No frame will point up the beauties of a painting as well as a check. Money paid down enrobes the painter in a garment of spiritual dignity, of professional excellence, of moral worth. It was a little girl who taught me this. She was sitting for her portrait and being very disagreeable. I said to her: "If you don't sit still, I won't be able to finish your picture." She said: "If you don't finish the picture, Mother won't have to pay you for it, will she?" She did not sit still. I was not able to finish the

picture. Mother did not have to pay. After that I
made a practice of asking for half of my fee in
advance. Thus the fathers were suitably impressed,
the mothers were disciplined, and the children
were always remarkably well behaved.

As the body of the painter's sales grows, the
public's confidence in him becomes firmer and his
prices become established in a more regular manner. If this takes place in a painting center like
Paris, his price quotations will have an international character. If in the provinces, his prices will
be established only for that local neighborhood
and the painting itself will not be exportable out
of the local region.

Georgia O'Keeffe and John Marin, whose pictures command such good prices in America, and
Duncan Grant and Christopher Wood, who sell
for such high prices in England, are almost unknown outside of their native lands. Even the
painting center itself occasionally produces figures
of purely local interest. Vuillard is almost unknown outside of France, although Bonnard,
whom he very much resembles, is known all over
the world. Signac is better known in France than
elsewhere although Seurat — of the same school
— is everywhere celebrated. To us here the name
Suzanne Valadon means nothing. But the pictures of her son, Maurice Utrillo, are in every self-
respecting house in Hollywood. On the contrary
both Pierre Roy and Marcel Duchamp are better
known here than in France.

Countries often manufacture for home consumption products that do not travel easily or are not liked in foreign lands. This happens frequently in literature. For example, André Breton has enormous influence outside France; Paul Éluard, of the same age and of the same school, is much admired in France and known only as a name elsewhere. Leon-Paul Fargue, Max Jacob, Mallarmé (save only for *L'Après-midi d'un faune,* which after all we only know as a piece of music) José-Maria Heredia, Richepin and a score of others, are unknown out of France; but Verlaine and Baudelaire have traveled very well. Maurice Rostand and Jean Cocteau have almost equal reputations in Paris. Rostand is unknown abroad. Cocteau travels because of his association with "la mode." Writers are often exported for reasons different from those which make them interesting at home. Anatole France is admired in France for his conversion to socialism, Balzac for his picture of French society; but in foreign lands they are read as scandalous, even as dirty, authors. Just as in somewhat the same way the red wine of the Burgundy region is altered for exportation by the addition of sugar for the German taste and of carbonation for the British.

However firmly, nevertheless, the painter's prices are established, as long as he is alive the n/m factor of my formula is subject to variations. The painter may "lose his talent" (the thing itself never happens; the phrase means "go out of style") or he may flood the market. Until the n/m factor is somewhat fixed and made constant by the painter's death and apotheosis, his market prices — not his fees as a professional man, but the value of his works on the picture exchange — are liable to uncertainty.

Against this uncertainty, many painters have in these last decades provided themselves an artificial death and a premature apotheosis. Marcel Duchamp, the greatest of the cubists, stopped painting entirely many years ago. Although he is himself a poor man, the market value of his work is tremendous, and I seem to see every three or four years a picture of his I had not known before. Picasso, like his musical counterpart, Stravinsky, employs the formula of a complete change of style every several years. The pictures of any particular period are known and numbered, and the market prices cannot be upset by additions. Giorgio di Chirico died against his will. His early work is as much admired as his later work is disdained, and he is reported to be under the necessity of forging his own signature.

In France there is a customary device of apotheosis by steps that is well understood and practiced. The canonization department of French picture buying has three heavens. The lowest one, whence comes the rain and the hail (and where sometimes pass the minor deities), is the Petit Palais. There, or in similar halls, painters who are beginning to be known are exhibited under semi-official government patronage. The middle heaven, the Luxembourg, is the Elysian fields. There abide the heroes, yet alive or but recently dead, awaiting the confirmation of their immortality. The firmament of the sun and the eternal stars is the Musée du Louvre, which houses the great and immortal dead. Thus three stages of apotheosis: promise, fulfillment, and masterpiece.

The Museum of Modern Art in New York is just such a machine for apotheosis. It tries to contain all three stages under one roof, but existing as it does in the provinces (New York is many things, but it is not yet a painting center), it finds the necessary exercise of flair, the forecasting of the present, as difficult and as uncertain as the forecasting of the future. Consequently it works best among artists already known by everybody to be great. Although it tries to atone for its lack of flair, normal enough in the provinces, by a certain academic seriousness and a scholarly approach to modern art, it is not really in on the ground floor. So it is likely to pick as winners the runners who most resemble the winners of the past when, as everybody knows, the masterpieces of today will differ in every possible way from those of yesterday and will not even look like art. The museum functions best as a hall of fame for the recently dead, a library of films, and a center for industrial design.

Most of the provincial museums, since they must take as models one of the three steps of apotheo-

sis, imitate the Louvre. And they do it very well.
Their pictures will be brighter, better chosen, better framed, more visible, better hung, and better
lighted than those of their illustrious prototype.
For the provincial museum is probably newer and
has fewer restrictions and younger minds. Although their setup provides for no Petit Palais
or Luxembourg, they are, nevertheless, likely to
feel a certain responsibility toward contemporary
painting, and will have a certain amount of money
to spend on its purchase and collection. And that
they do very badly. They have little contact with
painting as it is made. Their training is scholarly
and traditional, all about painting that has already become art. Consequently, they are confused by the lack of authoritative scholarship in
the contemporary field. They are accustomed to
the firmly established values of the old masters
and find themselves very much out of their ele-
ment among the jumpy market prices of modern
pictures. Consequently, they will buy the most expensive on the assumption that the most expensive are the most sure. In this way they can also
get rid of their funds quickest, and will be forced
to make up their minds, say, only three times instead of fifteen. So the cellars of the provincial
museums fill up with the discarded modern acquisitions of former years. More wisely they often refuse to buy modern pictures at all but will accept
them as gifts, thus putting the responsibility for

the possibly doubtful taste of the purchases on the shoulders of their benefactors.

The most useful service any museum can render the painter is, of course, to exhibit his pictures. A friend of mine once defined a painter as a man who lived in a studio and sent pictures to shows. This is not entirely true. Many painters do not live in studios. But all painters send pictures to shows. Showing his pictures is very important to the painter. Even by showing them to a casual visitor he can see them through other eyes, find out how his work looks to a stranger, get an idea of what a picture will be like when it is finished. No picture, however, is ever really finished until it is sold. At that point it ceases to be a part of the painter's private life. It has become public, external, something he can no longer paint on or fiddle with. The painter can look at it as if he were a cold outsider and make up his mind whether he likes it or not. Public exhibitions perform somewhat the same service for him. The pictures are framed, on a wall, looked at by a varied public. The painter can see his work through the spectators' eyes, judge his pictures' style and carrying power, find out what they are all about. After that he can go home and paint something different.

The sort of exhibition all painters prefer is the one-man show. Here the painter will present all his presentable work of the preceding two or three years. The one-man show, however, runs the danger of being monotonous because the painter will have been occupied since his last one-man show in painting different aspects of the same picture. And all the pictures of the exhibition, with all their superficial variety, will be fundamentally the same. A well-staged group show of two or three painters whose work combines and contrasts properly is always more varied and more interesting. A more common formula is the big show — the salon, the independents, the Carnegie and so on. Here the painter has a rather special painting problem.

Under ordinary circumstances an easel painter when he paints a picture has in mind a room in a private house as its final home. For that end he will paint his picture with a focusing distance of six to ten feet (that is to say, that the picture is to look its best from that distance), he will design it to be as interesting as possible for as long a time as possible (it must be lived with; it will be looked at again and again), and he will try to make it as little upsetting as possible to the decoration of the room where it will go — a room that will certainly have been decorated long before the introduction of the painter's picture. All this is a question of making an intricate and subtle pattern with not too much insistence on broad masses and simple colors. Such a picture, however, will be completely lost in any big show. So the painter who paints with the big exhibitions in mind must

do just the contrary — he must paint a large picture with a focusing distance of fifteen to thirty
feet, in strong colors and simple masses, and with
a pattern that can be quickly understood. Subtlety
and hidden charms are not very useful: the picture will not be seen very often, and it must be
possible to understand all of its qualities at a
glance. He must make something that can be
seen from across the room and that will outshout
any other picture on the wall. The product is naturally unsuited for private purchase, and if sold
can only find a home in a museum, a very special
market. I do not mean to imply that pictures
painted with the big expositions in mind are in
any way inferior to any other sort of pictures. It
is simply that they belong to a special kind of
painting intended not to be lived with but to be
seen among other pictures in a large room and
from a great distance — to the genre "masterpiece."

Carrying power and high visibility are perfectly
legitimate technical problems that any painter
should be able to tackle. But the problems presented by the sort of exhibition sponsored by a
nationally advertised product — such as Pepsi-
Cola, for instance — are not so legitimate. In an
exhibition of this sort, the prize-winning pictures
will be reproduced in booklets and catalogues.
This literature, together with publicity about the
exhibition, will be used to persuade the public
that the company which has organized the show

is benevolent, disinterested, artistic, and cultured. Consequently, the actual problem of the painter who competes is the problem of painting for reproduction. Neither paint quality nor carrying power is important for this. Paint quality cannot be seen through the medium of a color print, and carrying power is not necessary in a catalogue that will be looked at from only a reading distance. The subject matter and its arrangement on the canvas are the only things that count; these are the only things that will come through in this sort of reproduction. The company is eager to promote its good will with a large, literate, and presumably — since it is interested in contemporary painting — a politically liberal public. For that reason the company would like to appear to be liberal itself and not unappreciative of advanced sociological ideas. On account of the very nature of the painter's art, a picture with even the most subversive subject matter cannot be explicit or detailed enough to be actually dangerous. The more sensational the exhibition proves to be, the more publicity the company will obtain. Consequently, the more violent and the more shocking (within, of course, the limits of sexual respectability) is the subject of the painter's picture, the more likely he is to win a prize. So that painting for an exhibition sponsored by big business offers something that is more of the nature of a moral problem for a poet than of a technical problem for a painter.

Be that as it may, the big show is an admirable

institution and a useful outlet for the painter, provided that its entry is either open to all, as are the "independent" shows, or by invitation, as the Philadelphia Academy show used to be. But the jury show (where a jury that also awards the prizes decides whether the work submitted is good enough to be included in the exhibition) is an imposition on the painter and a menace to his already insecure position as master of his own profession. That a jury should award prizes is perfectly proper and nobody objects to it. God makes the rain to fall also upon the sea. But the invitation to submit his work, as if he were a student standing an examination, to a body of puzzled laymen or of certainly hostile other painters, no mature or self-respecting artist can accept. He is asked to deprive himself of his most important piece of work at a time when it is possibly more useful for him to have it on hand, to buy it a frame, and, if he does not live where the exhibition is to be held, to pay for its packing, shipping, and insurance — all in the vague hope of a prize and in the almost certainty of having his picture returned to him at his own expense, unhung. He is sticking his neck out, and he has no assurance whatsoever that the headsman's ax will fall for any responsible reasons. Here I step out of my role and make a special plea to the trade. We, as painters, must not so carelessly abandon our professional sovereignty. No self-respecting member of the painting profession should allow himself to be persuaded to submit his work to the judgment of any jury for admission to any show.[1]

As I have said before, a painter either makes his living as a professional man working for a clientele or he is supported and encouraged as a possible and future gold mine by a dealer and his cli-

[1] As an example of this sort of exhibition I will quote from the prospectus of the Southern States Art League for the winter of 1943–4. (The fee for the privilege of summitting a picture to the jury was five dollars.)

"Lists of prizes, as yet incomplete, show the customary annual awards in the field of the graphic arts — Miss Lila May Chapman's purchase prize of $25.00 for the best acid-bitten etching, Vice President Edward S. Shorter's block print prize and Grover Page's lithograph prize for $10.00 each, with a $5.00 award for a print in any medium offered this year for the first time by the Dallas Print Society. The Dallas Museum of Fine Arts will give a $50.00 War Bond, and Mr. and Mrs. Rufus McClung of Dallas a $10.00 cash award for work in any medium. In addition the Mint Museum of Art, Charlotte, N.C., is offering once more a purchase prize of $50.00 for the best watercolor. . . .

"How the League can aid both artists and patrons of art is illustrated by a transaction just completed. Last fall, Mrs. H. C. Dwelle of Charlotte, N. C., member of the Board of Directors of the League, wrote headquarters to find out if a painting, 'Sharecroppers' by Knut Heldner of New Orleans, shown in the 20th Annual Exhibition held in the Mint Museum of Art in 1940 were still obtainable. Finding that it had been sold, but that the artist would paint a replica, she commissioned him to do so, or, at his discretion, to paint another picture of similar subject and spirit, which she described as a 'touching Holy-Family tenderness.' When, at the end of December, she received the painting in its frame, carved by the artist, — a study of a man driving a shabby cart, and holding over his wife and baby to shield them from sun and showers alike, a small sapling cut by the roadside, she declared that she liked it even better than the first version, which had a more conventional umbrella in the father's hand, in place of the sapling actually seen by the artist when he met this foot-loose family on a Southern road during the depression."

ents. This last is where the glamour lies, and many a painter quietly painting the local gentry in a small town, or unhappy in an advertising agency, or even being rich and painting at home, longs for the big time, to be quoted on the stock exchange, to have his name in light, to become a style and an institution. Hungry for fame, he cries, "Where can I get a dealer?" I do not know, for the dealer is a very rare bird, combining, as he must, the best qualities of the clairvoyant, the devoted friend, the bunko steerer, and the stock-market manipulator. When painting is bought for its subject matter a dealer is not needed; he is nothing but a simple go-between, and the painter himself, or his wife, generally has enough business acumen to get along without him. But when painting is bought for its future as art, the dealer is as necessary as the press agent for the actress, the slogan for the cigarette. The models and predecessors of our present-day dealers were Durand-Ruel and Ambroise Vollard, who saw the possibilities of the unknown impressionists and made a fortune out of them, through whose hands passed all the great of their time, whose flair was impeccable, whose faith immense. A present-day dealer, however good, is likely to be less catholic. His career will probably follow something of this pattern: as a youth he will have fallen in love with the works of a small group of painters, all only slightly older than himself, and whose painting has been to him a revelation, a conversion to art. And he will spend all the rest of his life in their company. If he takes on a new painter, it will be one whose work resembles what he already loves. It will be a substitute, an addition, something to eke out a meatless day. He will be more faithful to his first loves. So, painter, if you want a dealer, pick him young and train him yourself.

But that is probably not the way it will happen. Your friends will buy your work. Knowing you, they will see in your pictures qualities no one else can perceive. As your friends grow older they will become more important and their importance will give you prestige and, consequently, sales Your clientele will grow exactly as does a doctor's practice. Eventually a dealer will take you over, not to impose you on his own clientele, but to act as messenger between you and the faithful you already have. You will be loved for yourself alone, and every sale will bring your other loves. For nothing is admired as much as something for which money has been paid. Advertising will do you no good, however gratifying it may be to you to see your name in print. For you are in a field where everyone fears that every critic is venal and every favorable notice bought, and where no one will take the word even of his best friend but listens to the oracle of some small interior voice, seeking to divine where next the cat will jump. A good reputation in the art magazines will sell a few pictures to the museums, but that is a special and a limited public. And no one but the painter himself ever reads his notices in the daily press. A householder will invest in a Picasso because he knows that all his friends know very well that Picasso is the best. And Picasso's signature is always written very large and clear. But you do not have behind you, as he has, all the forces of modern salesmanship, or all the minds that invented, or all the prestige of modern poetry, either. Nor are you likely to have. Glory such as his, next time it is attained, will be for other reasons; nor can you predict its future nature.

Remember how it happened last time. Who for twenty years from 1870 to 1890 was the undisputed lord of painting? Whose work brought the highest prices? Whose painting of flesh was to all the world the most exquisite revelation of young loveliness the world had ever seen? Who, with his imitators, dominated the schools and furnished the saloons and barrooms of far away Idaho and Turkey and Peru with gorgeous replicas of melting and languid and sumptuous nakedness? Who was it that educated the public, controlled the exhibitions, and kept the impressionists and the great Cézanne himself in an abject and indignant obscurity? Who was it then who was the cock of the walk? It was Bouguereau.

The present-day world has almost forgotten he even existed. His pictures are hung in the obscure garrets of museums, or are shown in private homes, a little laughingly, as the vagaries of yesterday's taste. Almost no one remembers his name. The present cock of the walk has different feathers. It is a little late now to try to join his flock. Nor do I think it is possible to foresee in what plumage the phœnix will next arise. All we can know is that it will be with very fine feathers indeed. It has always been so in the past.

Therefore, painter, unhappy as you may be and hungry for fame, the best you can do for yourself is to sit tight and keep your eyes open and trust your friends. Perhaps the phœnix plumes they think they see on you are really there.

CHAPTER VIII

MODERN ART

"Did you get that motorcycle so you could deliver your pictures on it?"

(WESTERN UNION BOY ON BI-CYCLE)

I was very young — it was in 1913 — when modern art came to America. It shot up before our delighted eyes like a skyrocket, scattering fire balls and splendors — Picasso and Picabia, Duchamp and Brancusi, Kandinsky, Marc, and Metzinger, and a score of others. It was better than any circus. In a time of brilliant new fashions and new dances — the Castles and their Walk, the Maxixe, the Half-and-Half — there was discovered to us a fabulous new land that had for its national anthem *Too Much Mustard,* for its prophet Guillaume Apollinaire, for its professional bad boy Picabia, writing dirty words on his pictures in pieces of string, for its Alexander the Great Picasso, and for its Columbus and Leonardo Marcel Duchamp, the handsomest man on two continents.

Everybody knew about modern art. Alfred

Stieglitz organized his own American cenacle
with the best of the local contingent. The War
came and passed. We hung on our walls prints by
Matisse and Klee, read *Tender Buttons* to each
other and whooped with laughter over:

CHICKEN
*Alas a dirty word, alas a dirty third alas
a dirty third, alas a dirty bird.*

We took *Dada* to our hearts, finding the young
Tristan Tzara silly but fun, as he was, and Erik
Satie witty and very fascinating, as he still is.
And we all knew about it. We knew about it almost as soon as it had happened. Picasso's earliest
cubist pictures are dated 1909. They were shown
here in 1913. It is now 1948. His discoveries,
though it is a disputed point whether they are his
or Braque's, are now almost forty years old. We
have had them with us thirty-five years, more
than a generation.

Nothing has changed much since. The school
that can with some justice be called abstract art
can scarcely be called modern. It is not contemporary at all. Its inventors and most of its practitioners are all elderly men. It has its saints †, its mar-
tyrs †, its shrines †, its pilgrimages †, its schools
of theology and discipline †, and even its Sunday
schools for children †. But since that sanctity, that
theology, that discipline are so well understood
and so simple to acquire, present-day talent in-

clines toward being more than a little impatient with it. It has become too easy to do.

What makes modern art different from the art of the past is that it is based on the combination of two nineteenth-century discoveries — the one in the realm of technique and having to do with the unity of the paint surface of a picture, and the other in the realm of subject matter and having to do with the use of past styles as a subject matter for painting. Both discoveries had been known to everybody for some time. But Braque or Picasso or somebody else in Paris about 1907 combined the two, and out of that union came modern art.

The technical discovery had already been made by the impressionists. It is the doctrine of unified surface tension — that no matter what illusion of depth or space or reality a picture gives, a picture is after all an object and every square centimeter of that object must be equally interesting. Unified surface tension is the basis and characteristic of all good design of our time, from Degas to Le Corbusier, from Chanel to the B-29. (Francis Rose, the painter, once said to me, pulling out of his pocket a flat tin of Luckies in red and gold and green: "How beautiful that would be if it were only by Chanel." But that does not really belong in this place, for it is a story, not about modern art, but about modern advertising.)

Before the impressionists, it was enough if the image — the various objects depicted on the can-

vas — was well composed. The impressionists discovered that the surface of the picture must be
composed as well, that the texture of the paint
itself must be made interesting. The size, shape,
and direction of the brush strokes must not depend under any circumstances on the size or modeling of the object depicted or on its position in
the picture. They must depend only on considera-
tions of unity of paint surface. One must be conscious of the picture as an object, as a flat surface
covered with paint. Cocteau expressed it by saying
that after all a picture is not a window. It would
be more proper to say that a picture must be both
a flat surface and a window. No matter what indication of depth is made, holes must never be
left that might interfere with the unity of the
paint surface. Textures and paint qualities may be
used to tie the image to the surface of the canvas.
That is why Braque mixed sand with his paint
and why Picasso painted with newsprint and paper cutouts. To achieve more completely this unity
of surface, even the image itself may be sacrificed.
This unity of paint surface is the key, the touch-
stone, the difference between the new pictures
and the old. And a picture is a modern picture in
exactly the measure that it possesses an equalized
surface tension.

The wife of a picture collector, to whom in
those more heroic days I had just been introduced
as a young painter, said immediately: "Do you
paint in sand?" And when I admitted that I did

not, she turned and left me without a word. Because if I did not paint in sand I could not be modern, and I had entered her house under false pretenses. But modern or not modern, neither I nor anyone else can possibly have painted in our time without having had to face, and to solve as well as we could, the problem of equalized surface tension.

The ideological discovery behind modern art is that the evocation of a particular style of painting can itself be a subject for a picture. A painter can distill in an alembic, as it were, a school of painting, abstract from it its basic characteristics, and present them on canvas as a concentrated and superior essence — an essential oil of art. The idea was discovered, I think, but not fully exploited, by the English pre-Raphaelites. A group of earnest young men, motivated by the greatest respect for the best in art and the highest principles of morality, they took as their theme the painting of Orcagna and Benozzo Gozzoli, which, I understand, none of them had at that time yet seen. The ladies of Shalott, their Gawains and Guineveres and Lancelots, were not actually their subject matter. Their subject matter was rather how Benozzo Gozzoli or Filippo Lippi would have treated these great figures if those painters had had the immense good fortune to have been acquainted with Tennyson's version of Malory and with Victoria's sobriety and good taste. Their subject was the evocation of the past. Their criterion for the excellence of their workmanship was how near it approached its composite and medieval model. Holman Hunt even invented an antiquarian way of painting in the oils that were not used in the period he was emulating. By laying down a thick coat of white lead on his canvas, smoothing it out like plaster on a wall, and painting into it while it was still wet with soft brushes and in drawing strokes, he could pretend that he was working in fresco.

But all this school was occupied with the emulation of only one model. We, on the other hand, may depict a variety of styles. Picasso has developed this idea elaborately, and taking as his subject a number of styles, each in turn, he has produced both pictures and a career of unparalleled brilliance. His early still lifes and cubist pictures evoke the essential forms and the multiple points of view and shifting perspectives of the mature Cézanne. The famous portrait of Gertrude Stein is a transition piece. It imposes on a Cézannesque body a head derived from Negro sculpture. (Picasso, after a number of sittings, was not satisfied with the head and took the picture to the country with him. There he finished it without the model. During that summer he began his next period, the one centered on the *Ladies of Avignon,* all about the Negro sculpture of the African west coast. As a result, the head of the portrait came out in the later style and quite different from the body.) The newer cubism of 1917, the *Harlequins* and so on, is a pictured representation of the costumes he had made for Erik Satie's ballet *Parade,* which evoked walking New York skyscrapers. There is a period of fat ladies whose weighty curves are derived from the classicism of Ingres and from the frescoes of Pompeii. The more recent sun-faced figures and women with two heads come certainly from an inspection of early Italian and Spanish tarot cards and the Byzantine frescoes of his own Catalonia. Very little uncertainty remains any more what his pictures are about. The objects depicted are for the most part plainly visible and what the titles say they are. There is even a sculptured head in bronze that is, plane by plane, the exact replica of the subject of several of his more disintegrated paintings. But his actual subject has never been, since the jugglers and mountebanks of his blue period, the objects on his canvas. His subject is rather how some particular school or race or time would have envisaged those objects.

Marcel Duchamp, too, comes out of the evocation of the style of Cézanne. But his work is not yet, even now, completely explained. His titles would lead one to suppose that his pictures have a futurist tendency, that is to say, depicting motion. I have looked at them often and long, and though they are in my opinion the most beautiful, perfect, and extraordinary of all cubist painting, I can see in them neither nudes nor bachelors. And I am inclined to believe that his names for his pictures are a sly wit, like his surrealist post card — the photograph of a sealed flask containing exactly (and since it is by Duchamp I am sure it is exactly) fifty cubic centimeters of the air of Paris and whose contour, taken together with its shadow, brings to the mind the shape of the human bottom.

Paul Klee, one of the finest abstract painters and one of the few modern Germanic artists — he was Swiss — of any great interest to the West, seems to have specialized in the ideology and perspective found in the drawings of children, and in doodlings associated with bushman churingas — those stones with labyrinthine designs supposed to contain the soul. He is the only one of the European moderns whose major work is not in oil. His color is superb; his titles are curious and amusing.

Albert Gleizes made a system of scholastic training out of cubism, wrote textbooks on how the disintegration by multiple perspective was to be performed, and painted enormous pictures to demonstrate it. Braque followed or preceded Picasso in many of his periods, and it is always a disputed point which of the two invented some of the modes. André Derain, who invented a sort of naïve village sign-painter's style derived perhaps from some of the more wooden of the Cézanne portraits, scarcely belongs among the abstract painters, nor do the other moderns who have followed the different aspects of Cézanne or elaborated on the Fauvism of Matisse.

There is a later group of men who are apparently occupied with experiments in shape and proportion alone. There is the late Mondriaan, much admired by the architects and industrial designers on account of the perfection of his rectangular proportions. And Hans Arp whose titles are joking and obscure enough (at one time he was exclusively occupied with the subject of bottles and navels), but who in my opinion is one of the greatest living sculptors. Generally, however, in all modern pictures there is an object depicted, though just what it is is sometimes difficult to determine on account of the obscurity of the painting style or on account of a purposely misleading title.

That is abstract art. And though I have not attempted to make a complete list of the abstract painters — that can be found in textbooks — you will notice from even the few examples I have cited that abstract painting has little to do with abstract idea. It is rather a transposition of the basic pictorial subject matter of painting — a change of key, so to speak — into a more remote plane. It is the evocation of an art style of the past or the depiction of an object clearly enough for the painter, the identity of which, however, is a secret not shared with the spectator.

There is a curious fact that has, perhaps, little bearing on all this: unlike the poetic painters, who form the other branch of modern art of which I shall presently speak, and who have very unruly lives indeed (for they must share with the poets

their restless search for subject matter), the abstract painters, for the most part, have correct and
domestic tastes in love and are either happily mar-
ried or tended by a series of mistresses. And it can
be supposed that the unexpected, the irrelevant,
the dangerous, and the untidy are banned from
their home lives just as they are from their pictures.

There is another curious fact. Since its first in-
ception, abstract art has had the firmest support of
the intellectual world. This would lead one to suspect that the subject matter of abstract painting —
the evocation of a variety of different styles of
painting — is a poetic device; and that the abstract
painter is more interested in illustrating a poetic
idea for the poets and in keeping them enter-
tained than in solving for himself his own visual
and technical problems.

The other branch of modern art practiced by
the younger painters has a more frankly poetic
subject matter. In this school are Salvador Dali,
Max Ernst, Eugène Berman, Pavel Tchelitchew,
to mention only a very few. Like the poetic painting of all times this school has the enthusiastic
support of the literary men, who with their brilliant — but to a painter, somewhat limited — intelligence, have no difficulty in understanding its
imagery — especially as this imagery is their own.
You will remember how Huysmans found in the
works of the painter Gustave Moreau a perfect de-

piction of the romantic decay and made him the
favorite of his *fin de siècle* æsthete, Des Esseintes.
And how to the teacher and philosopher Ruskin,
the pre-Raphaelites were an exemplary reappearance in England of the medieval skill, guild, and
past. Both subjects, romantic decay and medieval
revival, were of great utility to the literary men
because both were also subjects of immense interest to the rich of the time, occupied as these were
with the proper education and suitable housing of
their souls. (For the late-romantic soul had to be
cultivated, in the northern countries by the practice of travel, experiment in the sentiments, luxury, and despair, and in France by *"calme, luxe et
volupté.*) Our own poetic painters of today have
as subject either the young or the poor, or the fa-
bles of dream interpretation — both subjects pleasing to the rich of our own time, who find nothing
as touching as the contemplation of poverty from
a reasonable distance, and nothing as expensive
and impressive as the analyst's couch.

The poetry of the poor comes mostly out of Picasso's juggler family, and has been most taste-
fully exploited by Eugène Berman, Pavel Tchelitchew, and Christian Bérard. Berman's nostalgia
is for an Italianate past rather than for poverty,
though there is generally a beggar in rags somewhere in each of his pictures. He has had his greatest success in New York, where on the oak-pan-
eled walls of many a Park Avenue apartment he
provides a reminiscence of Le Nain and Piranesi.

Gertrude Stein was one of his first advocates and
admirers. Tchelitchew, perhaps the greatest talent of them all, admits a certain evidence of sex
among his poor. Although he is now extremely
successful in New York, his greatest success has
been in London, where more easily than in Paris,
which knows all about sex, or in New York,
which is very careful indeed, the slight equivoca-
tions of his subject can be passed off on the
grounds of art. His poetic backing has been the
Sitwells. Bérard, who was discovered and advertised by Cocteau, is little known in this country as
a painter. Although the fashion magazines for the
last ten years have been full of his drawings and
their imitations, few of his paintings have crossed
the Atlantic. Of the three, he is the most direct
descendant of Picasso's *Blue Boy*.

Freudian mythology has been treated by any
number of minor and by some major figures. At
the present moment it is more common a subject
in America than in France, where, I am told, it
has almost disappeared from painting. Among its
most important exponents are Max Ernst, Yves
Tanguy, and Salvador Dali. However neither
Ernst nor Tanguy is a pure case. Ernst, who has
the most extraordinary invention of textures and
paint quality of our time, paints by preference minor magics and small Germanic demons. Some of
his most beautiful work has been done as an evocation of the style of nineteenth-century wood-
engraved book illustration. Such is his *Woman*

with a Hundred Heads. Tanguy, an almost purely abstract painter and a very good one indeed, ties the Freudian subject matter to his pictures by means of a series of provocative titles. (A picture that looks like a small explosion on a beach is called *Mama, Papa is Wounded.*) Dali, however, does paint dream interpretation. As a young man new in Paris, he received much help from the surrealist group. The surrealists, contrary to popular belief, are not a painting movement at all, but a purely literary manifestation. They still exist, are still organized and directed by the French poet, André Breton, and are still occupied with the same things they were occupied with in 1924 — the excessive metaphor in poetry, the use of the unconscious mind and automatic writing in literary composition, and the political theories of Leon Trotsky. They have always had some painters with them, more as private illustrators than as leading members of the party. Dali was made much of by them until his desertion and excommunication about 1939. Whereupon he became his own poet and his own press agent. (The surrealists in the meantime became artists themselves and manufactured "gratuitous surrealist objects," which they offered for sale.) Dali's painting technique comes by way of the academic painters of Madrid straight out of Holman Hunt, Burne-Jones, and the other English pre-Raphaelites. It is clean, minute, precise, and detailed and is apt to look like a miniature landscape in a vacuum bot-

tle. His variations on his subject, Freudian symbolism, are of extraordinary luxuriance. His situation, of being at the same time both painter and
poet, is somewhat the same as that of Giorgio di
Chirico, and it is only by the most astute tightrope
walking, addressing himself by methods of high
pressure salesmanship to a richer and more innocent public than di Chirico himself could reach,
that he has escaped the same fate.

Di Chirico's case is an appalling one. He is a
painter of great talent and extraordinary gifts. His
book *Hebdromeros* is one of the curiosities of
modern French literature. His painting itself is
mostly concerned with a strange mixture of Roman antiquity, eighteenth-century grandeur, and
the domestic household objects of his Italian childhood. He was heralded by Cocteau and acknowledged a great painter by all the world. In 1929 he
designed for the ballet the sets and costumes of
his superb *Le Bal*. There he put all of his poetic
symbols: his gladiators, his seas in the drawing-
room, his horses, his dress-model women, his as-
trologers. Tired of them, I suppose, he began to
paint another subject. It was decided that he had
lost his talent. He was thereupon driven out. He
has never come back.

It is a curious and unexplained fact that the
poetic painter succeeds in stage design as no one
else can, perhaps because he has acquired a facility for illustrating poetic ideas. Christian Bérard
is, I should imagine, the greatest stage designer in

the world. His sets and costumes, simple and unpretentious as they are, are unforgettable. So were Florine Stettheimer's sets and costumes for the opera *Four Saints*. I have already spoken of Chirico's *Le Bal*. The Russian ballet itself is beautiful and loved, in a great measure, because of the sets and costumes the poetic painters have made for it. Tchelitchew's dramatic use on the stage of lights and shadows and simple colors is unlike anything else anywhere. Dali's staging and side shows are the most amusing of carnivals. And Eugène Berman's stage designs are so sumptuous that there is no need — or even room — in them for any actors. It is also curious that painters who are not painting an explicit poetic imagery are not interested in designing for the stage at all. Leonid, perhaps the greatest painter of them all, whose pictures have never a poetic image but are only about the various ways the land and sea can meet, has never consented to do a stage set.

The serious objection that can be made to poetic painting is that it inspires little technical advance. New poetic imagery is obscure enough in itself, and it can always be expressed more easily and more easily comprehended if it is depicted — without the added obscurities of an advanced painting technique as well — in one of the already familiar painting techniques of the past. It was the impressionists who made the technical discoveries of the nineteenth century, not Gustave Moreau. He only practiced with an antiquarian hand and an unbelievable skill the glazes and scumbles of another day. It is Whistler's painting, awkward and faulty as it may perhaps be, that we find interesting today, not Rossetti's. For Whistler in his imitation was using a contemporary, an advanced model. Rossetti was retreating into the quiet of a make-believe past. The painting of Holman Hunt is an impasse leading to nothing. And Dali himself has been able to make no improvement on his master's appalling dryness.

There is another objection to poetic painting, especially if the painter is his own poet — that it is bad for the painter's peace of mind. He who practices it must be in constant fear of going out of style. Poetic painting is like placer mining. The painter may at any moment exhaust one pocket and then must spend worried weeks and months and years looking for another. And he has little assurance that the next pocket, if he does find one, will hold anything but a glittering fool's gold.

The life of the poetic image is short. It quickly becomes unfashionable and seldom, if ever, is revived as anything but a scholarly curiosity. The poetic image in poetry itself often becomes ridiculous soon after its invention. Think of Richard Crashaw's *Weeper* where the Magdalen's eyes are described as:

> *"Two walking baths, two weeping motions,*
> *Portable and compendious oceans."*

Or where, when a cherub has drunk of her tears,

> *"his song,*
> *Tastes of his breakfast all day long."*

Very elegant at the time, I am sure, but now practically a Donald Duck. And since the poetic image is for the painter only subject matter, only an excuse for painting, it is neither part of that general wealth of the world to which he is always busy adding, nor part of that new vision of the world which he is always busy seeing. The poetic image is only an idea, and the progress of its degeneration is fast. What begins as a style of painting becomes first stylized and then stylish. What begins as a proposition in ethics becomes first a mode in decoration and then a technique in advertising. How quickly did pre-Raphaelism sink through Burne-Jones to Beardsley and posters, cubism through the decorative style of a world's fair to triangular pedestals for the display of merchandise! How quickly did surrealism become perfume bottles and shop windows! No dress designer, I am sure, could find the inspiration for a fetching hat in the painting of Cézanne. But then Cézanne would not submit to the patronage of Zola either.

And that, I think, is the whole point — all the strength and weakness of modern art. Why it has conquered the world and why nevertheless its conquest is not a victory. Why, wonderful as we all know it to be, however sound the ideas and technical discoveries behind are, it still seems somehow amateurish. Why Picasso himself so seldom paints as carefully as his subject could require. Why, even after forty years, abstract painting is only an ivory tower and the home of a minor tribe. Why the great public has never actually taken it to its heart, and to this day cannot visit one of its sanctuaries without thinking of Hans Christian Andersen's parable of the Emperor's new clothes. It is because when abstract painting was born it was taken over by the intellectual world. Modern art has been weaned and reared and ruled by the poets.

Chapter IX

POETS AND PARASITES

> "My mother wants *me* to be an artist. But heck, I can't draw. I can't draw anything. I can't even draw myself."
>
> (LITTLE GIRL SPECTATOR)

WHEN a painter has an exhibition that sells, a novelist publishes a book that is read, or a playwright puts on a successful show, he is in danger of being very unhappy for quite some time. For he is awed by his success, and day and night he has running through his mind the words: "That was good. Can I do it again?" and "What will I do next?" And he can't do anything. His success has turned him inside out. He is seeing himself from the outside. And he won't be able to work until he is back inside his own skin again. Sometimes a rest cure will do the trick — or an un-rest cure. Sometimes he just has to wait until his success dies down and he is no longer famous and impressed by it. If he is too young or if the success lasts too long, he may never recover. He may be permanently sterilized, or he may be forced to repeat all his life that same play, that same picture, or that same book.

177

This is particularly true when his public acclaim is not accompanied by the esteem of his own professional body. Then the artist knows that he cannot repeat his success because it was due to an accident that has nothing to do with his professional training. He knows that he cannot possibly guess again where the cat will jump, and he is horribly scared. And well may he be. For the jitterbugs of culture heartily despise the man who has once failed to send them.

The most unhappy of them all during an attack of success is the painter. For within his own professional body he has little natural support. Whatever painter he actually knows as a man, he always loves, having with him the common ground of painting materials. (Just as the French of the most different social classes can always get together on the subjects of cooking, sex, or military service.) But the painter he does not know, he always fears, too conscious of the other's different approach to the visual world and of the rivalries engendered by the preferences of the poets and by the smallness of the market. And a solitary painter standing alone on the pinnacle of success is in a dangerous place — nowhere to go but down, and with no friendly hand to steady him.

That is why painters always live in groups: Picasso, Braque, Derain, Van Dongen, and so on — Monet, Renoir, Manet, and so on — Bellows, Glackens, Luks, Henri, Prendergast, and so on. You cannot name a painter who was successful

during his lifetime and who had a long and varied
professional career who did not have around him
in the most intimate relationship as personal
friends or as personal enemies other painters painting the same sort of things — an active group
whose combined work made a professional background against which his own painting could be
judged. That small home support, in lieu of the
general approval of the big professional body,
which of course he cannot have, enables the
painter to know that his work is all right and no accident. Then he can face success without fear. But
the solitary worker, neither attached to a professional group working out the same problems nor
embroiled with a professional enemy in quarrels
about who did it first — the Cézanne, the O'Keeffe
— has either no success at all during his lifetime
or lives in constant fear that the cat may jump
somewhere else, that tomorrow he may wake
up without talent — talent being in that sense a
subject matter approved of by the intellectual
world.

I am sure that in former times the painter did
not bother about his talent at all, and that the
mark of a good painter was that he was approved
of, not by the intellectual world, but by his own
guild. But when talent becomes confused with
subject matter, the intellectual world can step in
and become the judge of a painter's excellence.
Today the right to sanction a painter's claim to
talent has even been taken out of the hands of

the intellectual world. It has been usurped by the poets as their own peculiar right. And now the solitary painter is at the mercy of the poets who exploit his product without having any responsibility whatsoever to safeguard its production. So the poets, by the authority they now exercise as arbiters of talent, can seriously interfere with the painter's normal working life.

The normal working life of a painter is this: He gets a new idea. It may be any one of a great many different sorts of things — painting in an unexpected size or in a different sort of texture or with a new sort of composition, or a different combination of colors, or any new way at all of painting any variety of subject. The new idea will probably first appear, rather clumsily treated, in the midst of a group of quite another sort of work. Then the painter will become interested in the new idea and for a while paint nothing else. He will do it over and over, again and again, each time more skillfully, in different ways, sizes, and pictures, until he has mastered it. Whereupon he will get another idea. The ideas are not too frequent. There may not be more than three or four of them in a lifetime. But the new idea is the subject of those biennial shows which painters are so fond of giving. That is why all the pictures in a one-man show are likely to have a certain family resemblance. They are actually the same picture, and the group of pictures painted around the same idea is what is known as the painter's period.

Acquiring a new painting skill is also a very slow process. The painter must slip up on a new skill as if he were trailing a fox. I once heard Leonid explain how he mastered figure painting. One day he found he had painted quite convincingly a minute fisherman on a distant beach in one of his seacoast pictures. Then he did it again, in another picture. Little by little — and it took several years — he contrived to make his figures larger and nearer, until finally he arrived at painting figures in the foreground in front of a distant landscape. That is the way something new must always be taken into painting. A new skill cannot be adopted suddenly. It must be worked at, over and over, until it is thoroughly digested and has become another equally unobtrusive part of the painter's other skills.

If the painter permits them, the poets will seriously interfere with both of these processes — the acquisitions of new skills and the sequence of his new ideas. The poets will make the painter force himself, go too fast, bite off more than he can chew, exploit his minor mannerisms. If under the poets' guidance his show is a success it will not be because the painter has solved some pictorial problem, which the poets know nothing about and are not interested in, but because he has illustrated for them some ethical doctrine, praiseworthy enough, no doubt, but not really to the point. Since the poets actually do control publicity and can make that elaborate, modern, fearsome magic work, the painter who is aided by the poets is himself in danger. For a solitary painter alone among the poets, awed by them and dazzled by his too quick, too precarious success, based not on his professional qualities but on his poetic imagery, may get his working eye gummed up and stop being able to see. He may even have to become a poet himself.

It is evident that the great painting successes of our time have all had to do with poets. Picasso had behind him Apollinaire, Gertrude Stein, Max Jacob, Jean Cocteau, Paul Éluard, André Breton, to name only a few. It is to be remembered that Picasso's subject — the evocation of a variety of styles — is intellectually very respectable, more powerful as a subject than either tenderness, antiquarianism, or psychological nostrums, and is eminently acceptable to the literary world. Bérard had behind him the great poet-and-press-agent, Jean Cocteau; and Tchelitchew, the weight of a whole family of poets and publicists, the Sitwells. Dali was for a long time the darling of the surrealists, a complete college of poets. The periodicals *View, Minotaur, VVV,* were supposed to be run by poets about poetry. They appeared, however, to be turned out by poets about painting — as a sort of supplement of illustrations to their own works. I do not know whether the Ferargil gallery in New York is actually run by a poet. Certainly the publicity about the Midwestern school that it sells — Grant Wood, Thomas Benton, and John Steuart

Curry — seems to have been directed by the best local poetic sales technique — probably by an admirer or imitator of the enthusiasm of Walt Whitman.

Nevertheless, whether or not this is so, I do not think that you can name a single well-known modern painter who has not had some poet behind him. This is because the poets today have a profession but no business. Poets cannot write about science or theology, as did Lucretius, for the professional scientist knows more about science than they do, and no one at all reads theology. Poetry has even been driven from the stage; there is no dramatic poetry, and although plays are frequently written in verse, they are written with the intention of being read, not acted, are seldom produced, and are never attended. Of love, our novels discuss the problems and our movies the act much more entertainingly than do the poets, and as far as the usefulness of poetry to the public is concerned, I am sure that it is much less of an effort, and perhaps a great deal more effective, to hold a young lady's hand in the dark while watching a moving and enticing image than to read her a poem. Moreover, even the poets themselves cannot always write about love. After their first lyric youth they become tired of the subject and are left the possessors of an admirable technique and no subject — a department store with no merchandise and no customers — all dressed up and no place to go. They know, as no one else does, the affective meaning of words; how in the most enticing manner to say nothing at all. So consequently they find their most appropriate job where this particular talent is the most in demand: they enter into advertising and become the inventors of modern salesmanship. I have been told of a sign in the window of a Paris shop selling stockings: "Your legs are poems. Get them bound by Kayser." It was signed, I was informed, "Jean Cocteau."

Much less distinguished copywriters than he have had their poetic training. "Whiter, whiter, softly soaks clothes whiter, whiter, whiter" and "So round, so firm, so fully packed, so free and easy on the draw" may both lack a certain dignity of sentiment, but they are most certainly the work of competent poets. The most expensive and honorific of all objects commonly sold are handpainted pictures, and more than soap or cigarettes, contemporary painting is in need of friends and a market. It is a dangerous and adventurous field as well, demanding of the explorer who ventures within its mazes a sure taste, a subtle mind, and a nice eye. So the poets take charge.

Taking charge is seldom to the poets' pecuniary disadvantage. Poets have all known painters since their earliest youth. They all possess collections of pictures, most of them given them free or bought at the lowest imaginable price from their painter friends. It is not a negligible consideration that when they take command of the painting market they advance as well the value of their own collection.

A musician among my friends tells me of a visit the poet Paul Éluard paid him at his Paris flat. As the poet walked in the door he said: "First let me see your pictures."

Mind you, poets do not necessarily know anything about painting. But they are very sensitive indeed about subject matter. They exercise an almost theological strictness in its censorship and defend jealously the access to the channels of publicity against all but, in their eyes, the most worthy. If the poets were not organized the painter could treat them as he would any other client, even though they never buy a picture except at the lowest *"prix d'ami"* and are consequently as difficult and as capricious as any other deadhead. No one really loves anything unless he has paid for it and paid well. But since the poets are organized, they cannot be persuaded as private buyers or made friends with as individuals, but must be conciliated as a committee. A multiplicity of judges is always difficult to deal with. The painter must offend none of them. So the work the poets crown is likely to be as null and as inoffensive as any war memorial. And though for a few painters and a few styles the poets may procure enormous prices and worldwide fame, on the profession as a whole they are an encumbrance. For they usurp the painter's professional authority, force him into the depiction of dialectical intricacies, and pull him away from patient inquiry into the aspects of the visible world, which is his only true pursuit. And disapproving of a subject matter, how easily can the poets say, bringing terror into the stoutest heart: "So-and-so has lost his talent."

(Although the poets are the undisputed masters of publicity, they seem unable to turn publicity to their own advantage. Gertrude Stein, who was in her own words a "saint of publicity," and whose name is the most widely known of all the poets who have written in English today, even at a time when one of her prose works was having an enormous sale under the sponsorship of the Book-of-the-Month Club, was never able to sell more than one small edition of any of her books of poetry — about the same number of copies that can be sold of any poet who is known to the other poets, but not advertised to the general public.)

The other parasite of the painting profession is equally respectable. It is the art-appreciation racket. It works by the dissemination of culture. It functions mostly through the museums.

Some ladies of my acquaintance, making a journey by train, encountered a young engineer from Oak Ridge. They tried hard to make him talk about the atomic bomb. He would not, but taking a book from the seat beside him and showing them its title he said: "I will tell you instead about modern art. That is my hobby." They found it very interesting that one so young, so important, and so scientific could also be so artistic.

I find it very interesting, too. A hobby is either something you practice or something you collect. Stamps, for instance, cannot be a hobby unless you collect them or counterfeit them. And I am sure that a young man employed in the fission of the atom would not have the time, or the money either, to paint or to collect modern pictures. Perhaps he meant something else. Perhaps he was making a collection of the advertising literature of the modern museums.

At this point let me assure the reader that however much a familiarity with the names and pictures of the modern painters may aid his conversation at a dinner party, this familiarity is only a form of cultivation and is not a hobby. Nor does it constitute a picture collection. Neither is it in any way the practice of art in our time. And unless you commune by buying pictures, or are a part of the priesthood because — even if only on Sundays — you paint, you are not in any way a member of the church.

The young engineer had obviously been subjected to the art-appreciation racket. He probably thought that looking at a booklet was as much fun as painting in oil. And I am sure that he actually believed that in learning a few names and some æsthetic theories and in buying a couple of prints, he had become an accomplished authority on all art and a collector of paintings.

The art-appreciation racket has its musical counterpart, the music-appreciation racket, which is
taught in schools and colleges and is designed to
persuade all the world that the important part of
music is not making it, but listening to it, and that
the only music worth listening to is the standard
romantic repertory, which is for sale and can be
bought at any store selling records. It is just as
simple as that. It is a plague and a pest to the music makers and composers who are not on the acceptable list — and few modern composers are —
but it brings in vast sums to the companies making
the records. And it is a bore to the public as well.
For it enables the symphony orchestras to play
over and over, again and again, the same nine Beethoven and four Brahms, as devoutly as if they
were officiating at Mass. It is, you see, a machine
for the dissemination of a standardized product,
which works by persuading the public that the
standardized product is all there is to be had. In
exactly the same way, the aim of art appreciation
is to persuade the public that there are certain
standard pictures known as "art," and to sell this
art, not in the form of paintings, but in the form
of colored reproductions.

Art appreciation has not yet arrived at the perfection of music appreciation. Nor can it until pictures can be reproduced in color prints as satisfactorily as music can be recorded on discs. But its
purpose is exactly the same: to sell reproductions.
This it does by educating the public to believe that

man's whole duty toward art is the appreciation of pictures, and that when a color print has been sold the entire purpose of the painter has been accomplished. The racket is a menace to the painter, who has only paintings to sell, who shares not at all in the profits of the sale of a reproduction, and who, undersold by the reproduction, is in danger of selling no pictures at all. After a Van Gogh exhibition held some years ago at the Museum of Modern Art in New York, the racket worked so successfully that the entire country was filled with people who, because they had bought a portfolio of reproductions, were fully satisfied that they were patrons of art and because they were convinced that they already possessed the best, would never again be in the slightest way interested in spending their money on art, much less in buying a real painting.

Copies of pictures have always been made. People used to buy them to hang in place of the originals they could not obtain or afford. The copies sometimes cost a great deal of money and sometimes were very good. Occasionally the painter himself even made them of his own pictures. The manufacture of copies by copyists proved a lucrative, if minor, profession within the art. Nevertheless, everybody knew that copies were not as good as originals. "Slavish copy" has become in the language a commonplace denigratory expression. But "photographic reproduction" curiously enough means quite an admirable thing. For "photo-

graphic" brings to the common mind that the
camera cannot lie, and "reproduction" implies
the multiplication of the loaves and fishes. So the
racket would have us believe that to possess a photographic reproduction does not mean at all that
one has bought a "slavish copy" known to be inaccurate and not as good as the original. But it
would persuade us that in this color print one has
acquired miraculously, through the grace of modern science and technological progress, and at a
vastly reduced price, the thing itself. Which is in
no way true.

Actually the present-day color print is abomina-
ble. Not in color, scale of detail, size, value of
lights and darks, texture, or paint qualities does it
reproduce the picture it is supposed to represent.
It is impossible to make any sort of judgment
about a picture from the inspection of one of these
prints. For that purpose a good black-and-white
photograph is much more useful, although for this
even a black-and-white photograph is sometimes
of little real use. Some years ago there was a law-
suit concerning which of two pictures, the one
owned by a Mrs. Hahn or *La Belle Ferronière* in
the Louvre, was the original Leonardo. From the
photographs published at the time of the trial it
was quite obvious that the picture in the Louvre
was the original. But from the photographs in a
recent book by Mr. Hahn it is equally obvious that
the picture belonging to the Hahn family is the

original. It all depends on which photograph you take.

Just the same, black-and-white photographs of pictures have a perfectly legitimate place in art and art scholarship. They are invaluable to the student and the art historian, who could not possibly be expected to have seen, or to have available, every picture there is in his field. Besides, if the black-and-white photograph is large enough and has been taken by a skillful enough photographer, it actually looks like the original picture, and although it will not make any pretense of being a replica, it will, nevertheless, give a more accurate idea of the actual qualities even of the paint surface of a work than will any color reproduction.

It is possible, of course, to make better color reproductions than are commonly to be had. There used to come out of Germany color prints that were reasonably good. They were, I think, the exact size of the originals and printed with a great number of lithographic plates, one for each color the painter had used. Each plate was elaborately retouched by hand, so that the prints were actually a sort of lithographic copy of the picture and not modern or scientific or progressive at all. However, this method of reproduction requires such skilled work and is so expensive that it is scarcely possible for the racket to use. Nevertheless, a suitable process will be found. It is only a question of time. And the setup is all there awaiting its discovery. Once the proper technological progress has been made, art appreciation is prepared to step in and take the painters over.

A culture racket of this sort, of course, can work more easily here than in a painting center like Paris. Partly because in Paris more pictures are sold. Picture prices have always been lower there; the painter sells more and can afford to ask less. The American painter, on the other hand, sells fewer pictures and is forced to hold them back for proportionately higher prices. Partly because with more painters around, everybody in Paris knows the difference between a print and a hand-painted oil painting. They know that the reproduction will never increase in value and that the painting will. Whereas our public here has already forgotten the difference between the real thing and the symbol for it. Consequently, here in the provinces art appreciation is a real danger, particularly as it has behind it the prestige of the expensive luxury that oil painting has now become.

The most powerful branch of art appreciation, the one devoted to modern art and its reproduction, is a source of considerable confusion to a very large section of the public. In an earlier day, Clive Bell's "significant form" confused a great many people because the word "form" has at least four meanings — flat shape, three dimensional solid, pictorial composition, composition in sequence, as in music, and so on — and "significant" may mean anything you like. The modern branch of art appreciation confuses the public in somewhat the same way. Because art appreciation itself — with its natural but unfortunate dependence on pedagogical systems — has been confused by a too close attention to the theories of the Bauhaus (a school for art, architecture, and the techniques of the kindergarten that flourished in Dessau after the other war), which, with a Germanic thoroughness and scientific literalness, actually believed and taught that abstract art was abstract. And art appreciation has become very like the Boston lady who said so happily to Monteux after he had conducted the first performance there of Stravinsky's *Le Sacre du Printemps* (it was some years ago): "This will do away with all the music of the past, will it not?"

Consequently art appreciation has tried to make a separation between modern art and all other art. It has only succeeded in persuading the great public that modern art is abstruse, pretentious, and phony, and that any other sort of art is reactionary, provincial, or expensive. So that by now the mind of the great public is confused about all painting. It feels either superior or suspicious. And its purse is completely closed.

Not long ago there were many brands of cigarettes on the market. Drug stores used to have whole show cases devoted to their amazing multiplicity, brands at every price and for every taste. With big advertising their number has dwindled to about half a dozen, and unless one lives in cities

and goes to special shops, that is all there are.
This is exactly what is getting ready to happen to
painting. But the case is sadder. Cigarettes are only
a local and contemporary anodyne. Painting is an
important part of any civilization.

Art appreciation uses advertising with discretion and effect. It sends to all the schools and small
museums throughout the country its tracts and exhibitions of abstract painting and modern art. It is
nevertheless offering a product that the public of
the small cities, for the most part, does not understand. This public has perhaps heard of the *Blue
Boy,* the *Mona Lisa,* and the *Horse Fair.* It has
seen none of these pictures and very few others.
Educating this public to the appreciation of abstract painting is like buying an elegant hat for a
lady who has no clothes at all but the slip she is
wearing. This provincial public does not need abstract art, cannot use it in any of the living it is doing. But since abstract art is so well presented and
on such good authority, the local public concludes
that all contemporary art is abstract art and, since
the art it has been shown is generally in the form
of reproductions, the local public concludes further that contemporary painting is only color
prints. So that, although this provincial public is
well brought up, and consequently keeps its respect for this art because it is art, it will never
again spend its money on any painting that is re-
motely connected in its mind with that word.

I know a number of painters living in the prov-

inces and selling their pictures who manage very
nicely because it has never occurred to any of their
clients that what they were getting was art. These
painters are very careful not to let that idea enter
their clients' heads. For then the clients would begin to compare what they were buying with what
the modern exhibitions bring them and very
quickly would begin to be difficult. Thus, in the
interior of the country no local youth who is painting anything that can be identified as art can possibly earn a living at it. Although the country is
full of youngsters with energy and plenty of talent, after a few years of working at it with no one
buying, with no possible market in sight, and in
competition as they are with modern art and high-
pressure salesmanship, they are forced to drop
painting entirely and enter into some more generous profession.

If art appreciation does not help the young
painter, it does not help the established painter
either. The painter profits only by the first sale of
a picture. This first sale is the result of a personal
contact the client has made with the painter and
his work — either when the painter paints a picture for a client or when the client sees a picture
the painter has already painted and, because he
wants it, buys it. But when the art of painting gets
to be sold as culture and as public education and
not as pictures, the painter is likely to go hungry.
For art appreciation is in no way a merchant selling a painter's pictures for him. It deals in culture

and, at most, sells reproductions, booklets, and
color prints, whose profits go into the editor's and
printer's, and not into the painter's, pockets. The
painter is put in competition with institutions made
for the public dissemination of education and culture, which, being subsidized, can offer it free. But
the painter is not subsidized. He cannot give it
away. His only living comes from the sale of his
pictures. The New York Museum of Modern Art,
the most conspicuous and perhaps the most interesting of the American museums devoted to modern art, with its textbooks and traveling exhibitions, however good the intentions may be, can
only operate to raise the market value of the particular pictures it advertises, all of them painted
long ago and now out of the painter's hands —
perhaps in the collection of the museum's own
trustees.

If art appreciation's only purpose were to sell
reproductions to people who cannot afford the original paintings, unremunerative as it might be for
the painter, it would nonetheless bring very legiti-
mately to a great many people a pleasure they
could not otherwise enjoy. But art appreciation
also operates to plug names, boost reputations, sell
paintings, and turn painting prematurely into art.
And it is there that the painter is likely to find that
art appreciation is a racket. Because the pictures
for which art appreciation performs these services all belong to a very special and a very limited
group.

Old pictures have secure enough market prices. They are already art. They are already owned by somebody, and their transfer from hand to hand profits little by the admiration of the general public or by public education. About the younger painters, art appreciation cannot possibly know, nor could it manipulate them if it did. Their pictures have not even begun to be art, their market prices are not yet secure enough for art appreciation to operate on, and there is not yet any considerable body of their work in any dealer's hands. So appreciation concerns itself with some of the aspects of the painting done in the first two decades of this century. Of the work of this period, there are many examples in the collections of picture merchants and of trustees of museums. Appreciation's aim is to raise the prices of these pictures as quickly as possible and to establish them at old-master levels. These pictures are admirable pictures by admirable painters. There is no more doubt about that than that the romantic symphonists, whom music appreciation has made its own, are admirable composers. Nevertheless, these pictures do not constitute all of contemporary art any more than the romantic repertory constitutes all of music, and the indoctrination of the public about these pictures, as it is done by art appreciation, is in no way disinterested or catholic. For it takes professional judgment out of the hands of the painters and presents this very small and very special group of pictures and names as the only and

the best on the purely external authority of a ring
of professors, æsthetes, and collectors whose docu-
mentation and erratic personal preferences are derived, at the very nearest, as a third-hand, hearsay,
hand-me-down from the only real authority in the
matter — the sound knowledge of the painter himself about his own craft.

At a time when the Museum of Modern Art
was being very unjustly attacked for owning too
many examples of the work of the sculptor Hans
Arp, Alfred Barr, its director, was quoted as justi-
fying its policy by saying, in effect, that when the
Museum had bought the pieces (at prices ranging
from seventeen to sixty-eight dollars), they were
worth only a fraction of their present market
value. So, obviously, the Museum, as was fair
enough, had made what might be regarded as a
considerable profit. But the works themselves had
long ago left Arp's studio, and the museum has no
obligation whatever to share its profits with him.
We can only hope that if the museum again buys
works by Arp, it will be at the advanced market
prices, or at least that the publicity Arp has received will enable him to make other sales. But
this is in no way certain.

A museum of modern art is, as you can see, a
bullish market, fine for the collector, but with little to offer to the painter himself, except perhaps a
retrospective exhibition — a funeral of the first
class, which few, if any, can hope to survive.

At this point I hear a question.

"But Mr. Corot, don't you think, nevertheless, that it is wonderful of the museums to enable the people to see all this art?"

Let me ask a question in return. What is the proper function of a museum? Of a university? Of an art school? Of a picture dealer? The answer to that is easy. A picture dealer sells pictures. An art school teaches people how to paint and how to teach painting. A university is a repository of history. A museum is a reposity of instructive objects.

Let us visit a museum. First we pass through the turnstile and are counted. At some museums, I am told, even employees returning from lunch must pass through the turnstile and thus swell the figures of attendance. The number of listeners is very important to a radio sponsor. The number of people who pass by its windows is very important to a department store. But both the store and the sponsor have something to sell. If a museum were nothing but a repository of instructive objects, it should be important to its directors that these objects be reasonably easy to get at, and the number of people who pass its door need not concern them at all. However, since most museums, some more than others, are very much concerned with the gross number of their visitors, one is led to suspect that their directors, as well as being custodians of valuable objects, are also tempted to act

as sales managers or as publicity agents. And since
the pictures on their walls are not for sale, the directors in these other roles must be interested either in what they actually do offer for sale —
their colored prints — or in advertising celebrated
names.

There is considerable difference between making knowledge available and boosting reputations.
For example during the New York season a great
deal of music is available. Eventually almost all
the music that anybody is interested in gets played,
and by good musicians. When the same musicians
who executed all this vast repertory in New York
go on tour, they present a repertory that is very
limited. The musicians of, say, Atlanta will never
hear on the local concert stage the variety of music they could make for themselves at home. But
the provincial amateurs are only a small part of
the public and of little interest to the director of a
concert circuit. He knows very well that in the
provinces a variety of unfamiliar music would offend the large public that can be induced to buy
a ticket only on the condition that well-known
pieces played by well-known names make up the
program. The director of the circuit knows that he
is not selling music but names, and that condition-
ing the public to remember a name is infinitely
easier and more profitable to him than cultivating
its taste.

If a modern museum were occupied in cultivating popular taste or in encouraging painting, it

would try to promote the sale of real pictures. Because a picture by the most unoriginal imitator of, say, Picasso is more interesting to have on the wall than any reproduction of Picasso could be. The painting is hand work. It is alive, the painter has infused it with some of his own vitality. And it may not be such a bad picture after all. It may, by the passage of time, which often reveals hitherto unnoticed qualities, turn out to be a better picture than anyone had thought, even turn out to be a celebrated work of art. But a color print is a corpse; it can only deteriorate. Its market value also can only drop. And its presence on a wall is as depressing (or as vulgar) as would be a framed piece of paper on which was printed the symbol for twenty-five thousand dollars.

The color reproduction is, in fact, very like the treasury note. Both are a symbol for money value. Both have no value in themselves. But there is this difference. The treasury note has been issued against a certain amount of metal on deposit, and the more notes there are out against this metal, the less each note is worth. On the contrary, the more color prints there are in circulation, the more the original painting can be sold for.

Consequently, a museum that is promoting the sale of reproductions is not promoting painting, because it is not encouraging people to buy pictures from painters — which is the only way there is of keeping their art alive. It is plugging names and acting as an agent of resale — which does not

help the painter or aid in any way the practice of
painting. It is occupied in whetting the public's
appetite for famous names.

Painters, as I have pointed out before, do not
profit by the resale of their pictures. In France
there is a law, designed to curb speculation in pictures and fictitious sales among merchants, by
which the painter or his heirs receives a small per-
centage of the resale price of his picture every
time it is resold at public auction. Nothing like
this practice exists elsewhere. Even in France
painters do not profit from the sale of reproductions. Unless a painter copyrights his pictures and
reserves his reproduction rights — something few
American painters ever take the trouble to do —
he has no rights whatever over the reproduction
of his work. Letters, as physical objects, belong to
the person to whom they are addressed. But as
ideas they belong to the writer and cannot be
published without his consent. Painters have no
such rights. Indeed the painter has so few rights
that if someone is writing a book about him and
wants to illustrate it with reproductions of his pictures, he must get permission, not from the painter
himself, but from the collector who owns them.

Nor is it an uncommon practice of museums to
buy a picture from a painter, sometimes very
cheaply indeed, on the pretext that it is an honor
to be hung in a museum, and then make a considerable profit on the sale of its reproductions. This
they are in no way bound to share with the

painter, nor do they. Museums have even been known to buy a picture and sell the permission to reproduce it to an advertising agency. From such a transaction not only does the painter receive no profit, but some advertising artist loses a possible fee.

The position of the museum in Europe is much less equivocal than all this. European museums are operated on public funds. Consequently, their directors are responsible only to the public. Here in America museums are operated mostly as private foundations. In the older museums the directors are not easily diverted from their proper functions, to serve the interest of the charitable benefactors — these donors being for the most part dead. So the older museums can perform the function, just as they should, of being disinterested guardians of valuable objects. The funds of the newer museums, on the other hand, are administered by trustees who are for the most part the original donors and founders. Consequently, the activities of these museums cannot be entirely disinterested. Trustees of art museums are generally collectors of pictures in private life as well. It would be very surprising if a museum, under such circumstances and out of common courtesy, would not help a little in making more famous the famous names in the collections of its trustees, and in proving that, after all, the judgment of its trustees in matters of art is sound. Hence the museum plugs names, often the particular names that are represented in its trustees' private collections.

The result of all this is quite simple. A public indoctrinated in such a fashion cannot learn the history of painting or even the history of art. It can only become familiar with a series of examples chosen from the history of collecting. However, the history of collecting, although it is not the history of art, is nevertheless of great interest to the art historian. For, just as it is only painters who know how to make painting, it is equally true that it is only collectors who are capable of turning painting into art.

As we leave the museum we pass a counter where color prints are on display for sale, framed, spotlighted, and attended by the prettiest of sales girls. I know you will be tempted to buy a print. Take, let us say, a Van Gogh. It costs little here, but on your wall it will represent a large sum of money. Some other painter's work might represent a smaller sum. The print of an unknown painter you must not take. That would be spurious coin. Prints of the same size all cost the same; we may as well have the best. And color prints are not without their use. Put half a dozen of them on your walls. Invite your painter friends to your house, not once but often. On their first visit the painters will begin by admiring your prints, saying what good taste you have. After the third visit they will become uneasy. And in the end, if they continue to frequent your house, they will have been made so unhappy by these facsimiles of money and immortality that they will all have lent and given you their best pictures to replace them. Thus, by the investment of a very few dollars indeed, you will have formed the beginnings of a collection of hand-painted oils all your very own.

Chapter X

THE COSTUME OF LOVE

"That artist sure is fast!" "Can't
you talk English? It's *girls* is
fast. Boys is *mannish*."

(LITTLE COLORED BOY AND GIRL IN
CHATTANOOGA)

THE BANISHMENT of the nude from contemporary
art is curious enough to deserve notice. It has
played the very dickens with the sculptors.

The nude is sculpture's only proper subject. Animals, architectural ornament, panoplies of arms,
and vegetables — what in painting would be called
still life — are all very pretty, but for the sculptor
relatively unimportant. Anatomy is the sculptor's
science. If he is able, he lives surrounded by his
naked models, has them constantly at hand so
that at any moment he can consult these living
manuals, these walking anatomical diagrams, on
the attachment of a muscle or the progress of a
form. Even the clothed figure he has always
treated as a nude with a veil of cloth. In fact sculpture exists because of the assumption that the
naked human body is an interesting and a presentable thing. The history of this assumption is
worth going into.

In the Greece of classical times, nakedness was one of the possible forms of formal attire, corresponding somewhat in its upper-class and urbane implications to our own dinner jacket. I say this with some assurance on the authority of the historian Thucydides. According to him the characteristics of the civilized man are these: he lives in cities, he does not carry arms, he does not practice piracy, and he goes naked. There are, he says, Greeks still living in the remote parts of Greece who, like the barbarians and like the uncivilized Greeks of less-enlightened times, wear belts when they take part in public games. But a civilized man goes naked. Consequently, Greek sculptors, in presenting the gentlemen naked and the ladies sometimes naked and sometimes in a transparent and clinging dress, were simply copying a current costume of the period.

This convention was respected in the colder and more barbarian Rome as an exotic and somewhat, so to speak, "Frenchified" mannerism. And although nudity as a costume was admitted, it was considered more a gladiatorial than a gentlemanly costume, and the Roman gentlemen were for the most part shown in their portrait statues in their senatorial robes or military accouterments, and the ladies in the voluminous dresses of their rank. Nevertheless, there can be found in the Metropolitan Museum of New York a full-length portrait statue of the Roman Emperor Gallus, done in the third century of our era — a statue of a large man,

rather heavy around the middle, evidently an excellent likeness, and dressed only in his shoes.

But all this is depiction of nudity as a local costume, not the use of the nude as an erotic symbol.
The frankly erotic nude is older than history.
There are examples from the Cro-Magnon depos-
its. Its purpose, as an image of a god or as an in-
ducement to fertility, is always precisely indicated
— as in the Diana of Ephesus — by the character
of its attributes. But what I shall call the voluptuous nude in art, the nude evincing a gentler and
more generalized eroticism than this, is much
more recent. It was, I think, a Hellenistic invention. It appeared about the time when Macedon,
with its acquired taste for Asiatic comfort, had dis-
placed Sparta, with its tradition of military discipline and the simple life, from leadership in Gre-
cian affairs. The voluptuous nude was exported
in effigies of gods and goddesses, in pictures and
statues and cameos and terra cottas, on fans and
mirrors and jewels, on chairs and tables, on buck-
ets, wine cups, and perfume bottles, to all the
Græco-Roman world, as a symbol, not, I think, of
love, but of luxury and of Greek taste, of the amenities of ʻcivilization and of the pleasantness of
life. And wherever Hellenistic culture had spread,
the formal garb of nudity could be worn with perhaps the same sort of connotations and sentimen-
tal evocations of the past and of its grandeurs as
have our own ante-bellum gowns.

After the shift of the Roman empire to the east, Hellenistic art disappeared. Byzantium was exporting something quite different — an authoritarian faith — and had no use at all for the symbols of a paganism and of a luxury trade that it opposed. Under the direction of the church, the Greek, or perhaps Syrian-Greek, artists carried to the limits of the known world the symbols and attributes of royalty, of authority, and of godhead. The voluptuous nude disappeared. Very few nudes, and those very conventional ones, can be found in Byzantine art. This does not mean that the people of those times were unnaturally chaste, nor does it in any way prove that, then or later, nudity was banned as a public costume. Throughout the Middle Ages men and women bathed naked together in the public bathhouses, and in carnivals, municipal celebrations, and *joyeuse entrées* (which were festivals confirming the friendship and mutual rights of a sovereign and a town), the presence of naked ladies of both professions — the honest and the oldest — embellished the floats and spectacles. Painters after Cimabue did not hesitate to show Adam and Eve in their appropriate costume of nothing at all, or to depict the souls in limbo as naked. But they were using nakedness, not in its enticing, but in its functional, its storytelling aspect, as a way of presenting the primal innocence of our first parents or of demonstrating the cold and helpless discomfort of the damned.

There is not to be found in all the art of the Middle Ages (except perhaps as a symbol for the devil) a single example of the voluptuous nude.

By the middle of the fifteenth century public nudity had disappeared from Italy. A mid-century Italian humanist and letter writer, who certainly was no prude if one can judge from his taste in anecdotes, was shocked to find himself being scrubbed by a naked female attendant in a bathing house in Basel. A *joyeuse entrée* of Charles V in the first decades of the sixteenth century is the last time in Europe that ladies decorated a public occasion with joyful nakedness. At the beginning of the fifteenth century Greek learning had reappeared in Europe. The end of the same century witnessed the introduction of syphilis and the reappearance of the voluptuous nude in art.

It would seem to me that the grouping of this quatrefoil cannot be entirely accidental. If the voluptuous nude first appears in art by the agency of Greek learning as a symbol of a gracious and civilized and vanished way of living, it remains there as an allegory of the kinder aspects of the love, which in its physical reality was becoming, with the raging of the pox, more perilous every day. Reform engulfed the world. Passions were unleashed by ecclesiastical controversy. New churches were founded on the condemnation of priestly irregularity. Chastity was appointed queen of all the virtues. The voluptuous nude in art flourished. Lucas Cranach, painter of the most perverse and, to some tastes, the most seductive, of all pin-up girls, is an exact contemporary of the Reformation.

Of the three possible uses of the nude in art — as the depiction of an actual costume, as a classical reference, or as an erotic symbol — the last two have been most common from Renaissance times to our own. Nudity as a garb has appeared so little in public since the end of the fifteenth century that this use of it in art is difficult and rare. Of our own times Degas is one of the few painters who has succeeded with so treacherous a subject and by some extraordinary quality of mind has managed, in his *Spartan Girls Challenging the Spartan Boys to Wrestle,* to paint a historical scene as if it were a contemporary and everyday occurrence. Other painters of our time in a similar endeavor only succeed in showing us a professional model who is receiving twenty francs an hour for sitting still in, let us hope, a comfortable room. On the other hand, the nude as a classical reference or as an erotic symbol — as nymphs in a forest, as the rape of the Sabines, as Susanna at her bath, as Saint Sebastian embarbed with arrows — has been, from the time of Botticelli until the beginning of this century, the subject most beloved by artist, public, and client. If it became necessary, the erotic aspect of the nude could always be disguised, satisfactorily enough, in classical presumptions and in historical associations. And although the act of love, even under Victorian delicacy, could not be banished from private use as easily as could the nude from public converse, love could at least be treated under its more remote and spiritual and educational aspects. The poets themselves were not free from this infectious respectability.

Some fifteen years ago Robert Carlton Brown published an *English Poets Censored* after the model of *Mother Goose Censored,* a famous tract against literary censorship and, by blacking out a word here and there, rendered our familiar quotations from the poets so scabrous that, though I will quote some of them in the original, I would not dare to make a translation of them into the bowdlerese. That the reader must do for himself.

> *My love is like a red red rose.*

> *Just for a handful of silver he left us,*
> *Just for a ribbon to stick in his coat.*

> *Fell softly as an angel's feather*
> *Through the high ether silently.*

and so on. All you have to do is to mumble some of the words.

The pre-romantic poets were less changed by these mutilations. No substitution of a harsher word for "love" or "sweet" made any difference in the sense. For these poets mostly said what they meant and meant precisely what they said. The romantics were more vulnerable. No matter what word was blocked out from the text, their poems became fantastically obscene; as if no matter what subject they were writing about, they were nevertheless thinking about the act of love. This is perfectly possible for love had assumed an enormous and hidden importance. By the end of the eighteenth century, by the time of the beginnings of romanticism, in a world dedicated to respectability and to commercial expansion, love had become the most difficult, the most clandestine, and the most expensive of undertakings. The danger of disgrace in a world beset by respectability, and the probability of disease in a world still infested with the pox, had made love costly indeed.

Anything bought at such a price is infinitely tempting and its concomitants honorable. Although nudity as a costume was severely censored — William Blake was called mad because he said, wittily enough, to a visitor who found him sunbathing in his garden in company with his wife, "Don't mind. It's only Adam and Eve" — nudity in art was acceptable and admired and its erotic associations were painstakingly forgotten. Abstracted from love, nudity became the convenient symbol for any abstraction you please — commerce, agriculture, better government, mathematical genius, or the rights of women. It is an extraordinary thing that more acres of bare human skin were exposed by this most pudibund of all epochs to the cold winds of public inspection than by any other era since the Greeks and Romans.

All this is the past. In the first years of our century, about the time of the first World War, nudity appeared again as costume and the nude in art went out of style. The nudes of Picasso painted after 1914 are either the severest of classical references or exercises in calligraphic dexterity. Their bent-wire outlines or their tubular forms could not possibly be confused with human flesh. Matisse has done some nudes, but he has treated their bodies as a flat and neutral pattern, a point of rest for the eye, against the much more living wall paper that is really the subject of these pictures. Chirico painted a whole exhibition of nudes. He mistakenly attempted to make his ladies look ancient Roman by seating them on fragments of Corinthian columns. The subject he had chosen was so unfashionable at the time that it was instantly decided that he had lost his talent. Dali's nudes are either monsters or references to an Edwardian prudery — not human beings. Other painters of our time have either avoided the subject or schematized it or if they have treated it, they have all had with it an equal ill success. Nude statues and pictures of the nude, unless they are by such celebrated names that they cannot be spared, quietly disappear from our museums and from our public parks. The nude in art is gone. At the same time human nudity has become a great deal less opprobrious. Mixed bathing, in a brevity of costume that would have shocked our ancestors, is practiced at all public beaches, and in the state of nature itself at many private ones. Under the ægis of the Protestant church, of the very child of Luther and of the Reformation, complete nudity has been adopted as the costume for swimming in every Young Men's Christian Association in the land.

The sequence is closed. The serpent has bitten his own tail. Perhaps the connection is accidental; nevertheless, upon the advent of syphilis in Europe and at the time of the disappearance of the human nude from public life, the voluptuous nude appeared again in art. And now, five centuries later, the nude disappears from art and begins to be tolerated again in public life, at the precise moment when a cure for syphilis is put at our disposition.

Accident or no accident, today we find ourselves living in a safer world, where private lives are less exposed, where nothing that we can do has any cosmic consequences, where love-making is common and easy and somewhat despised, where the great bond of "two alone against the world" has been dissolved, where romantic love is unfashionable and true love concealed. The textbooks of abnormal psychology, which everyone has read, describe as abnormal even the simplest of human desires, and although everyone does exactly as he pleases, we all have in our minds as model and comparison, Case History No. 365, and we are all ashamed. All fashions of love-making are known and considered probable; no one wishes to expose his private conduct to public judgment. Consequently, people do not hang pictures of nudes in private houses. The implications, either positive or negative (for the presence of a nude of either sex on the walls of a private house either asserts or denies in the host a particular direction of erotic endeavor), are much too difficult to live down. For the same reason there is no sculpture on our public buildings. It might be carelessly assumed that a committeeman had an undignified taste for nude bodies. It is as if we all made love with our clothes on.

Thank goodness we do not. But nevertheless it is a noticeable fact, perhaps even a symptom of the return to a civilized condition that nudity as a costume, as it is worn today in Y.M.C.A.'s, in college dormitories, in private houses, and at beaches, is not at all a symbol of sex, but a symbol of innocence and of social equality, of Adam and Eve, and of the educated classes. One can undress before a friend, but not before a servant; the proof of the innocence of a college locker room is its unremarked nakedness. The nude as an erotic symbol has disappeared from our daily life. Its place has been taken over by photography.

The camera has an eye but no hands — it cannot feel with its fingertips, has no sense of touch or space or warmth. To it all skins are beautiful, all nudes voluptuous. It has its own canons of beauty. These we cannot escape. They crowd in on us in every movie, on every poster, on every billboard, in every magazine, these photographs of

young men with muscles and smiles, of young
women with bosoms and legs, all as nude as per-
mitted and all, to the camera's eye, beautiful. Nevertheless, this beauty is not beauty, it is sex appeal;
not art, but advertising, an exploitation of the public, a method of salesmanship. It is technically
known as "glamour." Everything that is sold,
from a chewing gum to a system of morality, is
packaged with this product of the camera's vision. It is the sugar-coating on the pill, the cello-
phane around the merchandise (a substance I
have seen in use in shop windows to guarantee the
virginity of such unlike objects as a grand piano
and a banana).

This camera's vision of the nude, this sex appeal,
is not in the least sexy, does not encourage the con-
gress of the sexes. On the contrary, it is autoerotic.
It is the idea each of us has of his own body as he
thinks of his own image in a mirror, and leads
away from love. We live in the midst of these
monsters of photography. They are always about
us. It is almost impossible for us to clean this dirt
out of our eyes. Just as in Victorian times the idea
of the nude body was inevitably connected with
the idea of shame, in our own time the idea of the
nude body (because the photograph is mistaken
for life) is inescapably connected with the idea of
sex appeal. So, to the voluptuary, who confuses
the pin-up with his own experiences, all nude bodies are exciting, while to the inexperienced, who
is shocked by the difference he finds between the

camera's vision and his own, all nude bodies are appalling.

If a painter or a sculptor of today yields to the oppressive canons of sex appeal, as do Vargas and Petty, his work becomes vulgar and commercial. For even if it is done with the purest of motives, it can nevertheless be easily used to add glamour to a sales talk. If he avoids these artificial strictures, his work, though it may appear imposing as art, will seem to everybody distorted and unacceptable. Nowadays there is no place any longer for the nude in art; we have too much sex appeal around us in life.

The painter can get along very well without the nude. There are plenty of other things he can paint, and if he must, he can fit the nude into the pattern of daily life, as did Degas and Bonnard, by painting it with a bathtub. But sculpture cannot get along without the nude, nor have I ever seen a bathtub introduced into a sculptured group.[1] The nude, or at least the nude figure with the thinnest of drapery, is the sculptor's only serious subject. His one subject forbidden, the unfortunate sculptor gets no orders. The art of sculpture is too elaborate and arduous and expensive to be undertaken as a private amusement; the sculptor no longer learns his trade. The ones who get the few jobs there are to be had, hide their inexperience

[1] I have been informed that there exists a Rogers group, formerly used to advertise Pear's Soap, of Venus washing Cupid in a bathtub.

under a professional-looking streamlining. The others do few and small pieces. It is a hard time for them all. Today is the first time in history when architecture does not use sculpture for its adornment. The empty niche has become a standard architectural ornament — and for quite other reasons than that of Ronald Firbank's queen, who found the empty niche "so suggestive."

Perhaps, nevertheless, the sculptor's luck is about to change. The study of Greek and Latin, once a gentleman's only education and the unique curriculum of every school, has almost disappeared from present-day instruction. Perhaps after four centuries of it, classical culture has at length been absorbed and digested. Very little of it nowadays remains strange or different from our habitual ways of thinking. Perhaps we are at length becoming civilized. We live in cities, do not, as private persons, carry arms, do not, except as corporate bodies, indulge in the practice of piracy. Perhaps presently we will also begin to go naked. The yearly shrinking of our already scanty bathing costumes promises progress in that direction. Nevertheless, nudity is not real unless it is complete. Nor can, with any justice, the Australian bushman be called nude who reduces his zone of immodest exposure to a point at the very tip of his organ of generation, upon which he clips the shell of a snail. He may not be as warm, but he is as clothed as any of us. If, however, we again begin to go naked, if nudity once again becomes a neutral and a presentable form of apparel, if sex appeal — as is possible — by its very abuse loses its power and disappears, then sculpture will resume its place among us as the greatest and the most permanent of all the arts. And the sculptor will again be able to celebrate what is properly his subject, not the classical associations or the erotic evocations, but the actual nobility of that animal which, we are too apt to forget, is God's sublimest work.

CHAPTER XI

PAINTING IN PUBLIC

"When will that picture come
on at the Tivoli?"

(ROSSVILLE MOVIE FAN)

I suppose the practitioner of any profession is always shocked when he sees in the movies how the public likes to envisage him. Doctors in the films are always young men whose main problem in life is deciding whether to have a chaste career in the laboratory fondling their test tubes, or to go out into the world where they will fondle the hands of a rich, older, but still extremely attractive, female patient. Newspaper reporters are depicted as gentlemen who continually quarrel with their editors, travel only by plane, and have an unlimited expense account. Opera singers in the movies are always running away from impressarios, instead of, as it happens in life, the other way around. Young long-hair composers arrive at fame through Tin-pan Alley. And painters are always rich.

Would that it were true! And that the other agreeable aspects of the painter's life conjured up by the movies were true also — that our models

221

were as pretty as those we are surrounded with in the films, that we lived in as luxurious studios, and that we sold our pictures for as impressive sums as we do there! (I have never seen a painter in the movies sell a picture for less than three thousand dollars.) There are other aspects of our glorification that we like less — we are depicted as artists, soulful and temperamental; we have dreamy eyes and long thin fingers; the pictures we paint, if one ever catches a glimpse of them, are invariably the most deplorable daubs, and our private lives are spent in the throes and clutches of romantic love. Just as the newspaper reporter of the films is not a reporter at all, but the much more glorious press agent, the lowly painter in the films is given a romantic sensibility and is glamorized into the æsthete.

We don't like it. We are not like that. We are a serious professional body doing a serious job. As individuals we possess only just enough sex appeal for our own private uses. Our lives may be a little more free (because we can travel a little more easily) than the doctors' or the lawyers' but no more romantic, and we are likely to harbor no more romantic illusions than does any other serious artisan.

This is natural enough. Since the art of painting first began, painters have always known how to do two very serious things, and have always been kept busy doing both of them: adding to the world's riches and teaching people how to see. Out of a few bits of cloth and wood, some oil, and colored powders, the painter makes his pictures. The materials are nothing; the picture is immensely valuable. Though the picture may temporarily lose its value because it has gone out of style, if it has ever once had the approval of other painters, it will always come back into style again, regain its value, and remain immensely valuable until it falls apart with decay. The perfection, elaboration, and character of this picture, this work of art, has always been taken as a record and a measure of the qualities of the civilization in which it was produced.

Besides creating wealth, the painter invents the visible aspects of the world and presents them in a dramatic form that everyone can see. That he can do because he knows how to see. His is also the only profession that knows about shape and form and proportion and color, and their use in making things be visible and look right. That he knows, not just because he has some bright ideas, but because he has some hard-gained knowledge from the work of making pictures. Consequently, one of his proper functions in the world is that of being the final judge of any piece of design. Whenever design has been good, that has been one of the things expected of him.

However, just because he is a painter, do not expect him to be all over the place, in everybody's way, sticking his nose where it does not belong, messing around with minor trades or inferior techniques. He is not a simple technician; he is the inventor of all these things. At such a repetitive and subservient occupation he would be a bore to everybody including himself. Nevertheless, I would like to see him regain his lost prestige. To do that is simple. All he needs is to paint and sell lots of pictures. Then he will regain his self-respect, he will again become the arbiter of taste, his profession will again be what it has been in the past, the noblest, the freest, and the most lucrative of all the crafts, and he can let the arts take care of themselves. And the painters, as a numerous and prosperous body, could make the world again into the visual-minded place that today it certainly is not.

I would not ask the painters to organize themselves into any restrictive guild. Remembering the painters I know, I do not think it could be done. Painters are too irregular, too disparate, too diversified. Besides, any organization of painters there has been in the past — except possibly the medieval guilds — has been the organization of one group of painters at the expense of the profession as a whole. The medieval guild worked because at that time there was an enormous demand for painting — by the state, by the church, and by private individuals. The whole profession was organized around the painter's training, for the specific purposes of protecting the painter from his clients and of assuring a high level of quality in the product the client had ordered. The present-day medical profession is organized in exactly the same way and for exactly the same ends.

Today, however, the demand for painting is small. Consequently, there is no reason for the guild to exist, and the painting profession has become, quite naturally, an unorganized group of great men and individual talents who have very little responsibility at all to any professional body or system of schooling. This is exactly what would happen to the medical profession if the demand for the services of the doctors almost ceased.

The composers are organized as a part of the union of performing musicians, over whom they exert a real, however distant, authority. But it would make no sense at all for the painters to join their nearest organized affiliation, the union of painters and paper hangers, who are not even aware of the existence of the artist-painter. Any organization of the painters done from the outside, say by the League of Young Republicans or by the Communist Party or by the Manufacturers' Association, I and many others would not accept. The organizing group would certainly be using the painter's prestige for its own ends, and not to serve the specific interests of the painter himself. Nevertheless, if any one would show me a scheme for organizing all the painters — broad enough to take in everybody, and directed against our common enemies — I, for one, would join it at once. But I do not think that today, with our small mar-

ket, such an organization is possible or even
needed.

Nevertheless, such an organization, in a loose
form, already exists. And every single painter,
whether he wants to or not, no matter what his
politics or his æsthetics, no matter who are his
friends or who buys his pictures, belongs to it.
And he belongs by the simple fact that he has
studied drawing in a life class and that he has
once sold a picture. It is the professional body of
painters.

But if this body is to work, the painter must act
as if he belonged to it. He must take his professional pride out of storage where he has been
keeping it, dust it off, and put it on at as cocky an
angle as he can. He must not again forget that he
is the same species of animal as were all the great
painters of the past, and that he is doing exactly
the same sort of thing they did before him. He
must realize that his profession, in spite of its apparent divisions, is just as solid as it has always
been, and that in spite of technological progress
— or even, perhaps, because of it — the painter's
clear eye and common sense are more needed in
the world than ever before. He must know that
yesterday or today the difference between one
painter and another is not of ideology, but of talent; that the schisms that split his ranks, the tur-
moils and enmities of modern art and publicity,
are not his own disputes, but the quarrels of his
patrons and exploiters; that the world is divided

for him, not into friends and enemies, but into friends and clients; and that the more producing painters there are in the world, the better off he is.

I have said it several times before, but it is still true. The more working painters there are, the more general interest there is in painting. The more general interest there is in painting, the more painting is sold. And the more painting is sold, the more producing painters there will be around and the grander will be the product they turn out. I have been told of a small Mississippi town that supports five or six working painters simply because their presence, their number, and their rivalries have excited public interest, where everybody buys water colors, and where all babies, all debutantes, and all mayors sit for portraits. This is, of course, a very provincial market indeed. But the same thing can happen in a larger town if the painters are active and numerous enough and interested enough in what each other is doing.

As I see it, the cause of all the painter's woes is that although there are elaborate and effective means of communication among the dealers who sell painting and among the poets who advertise it, there is practically no means of communication at all among the painters who manufacture it. So I would recommend to every painter the routine of getting acquainted with every painter he can possibly know, of making friends with him and finding out what he is all about. The painter is accustomed in these lonesome and ungregarious days to live in professional isolation surrounded by his few clients and friends from other trades. He will be surprised to find out what good fellows, how sympathetic, understanding, and intelligent his fellow painters are. And of course they are. They are all doing exactly the things he is doing, facing and solving exactly the problems he has to face and solve. And the differences of opinion among them, which appear political, are really only differences of subject matter and mostly encouraged by the poets.

This may seem a vague remedy for all our ills, and perhaps it is. Nevertheless, unless we painters maintain some system of easy communication among ourselves, we will soon lose what little we have left of our autonomy. Communication by means of the art magazines is liable to all sorts of censorship; the magazines are already subject to the appreciation racket. But direct communication between painters by word of mouth, if it can be maintained, cannot be censored at all. And communication between painter and painter, and between painter and public, is of immense importance to us all.

We lost our professional organization when the guilds finally broke up at the end of the eighteenth century. Today we are losing all the other rights of a professional body as well — the education of the neophytes, the privilege of final judgment on the product and control of its merchandising. I do not mind so much the loss of the guild and of the school. If any form of guild that would work with our diminished market could be designed, I think it would have been tried long ago. And I, who do not have a taste for teaching, view with alarm the effect that teaching regularly, day after day, has upon any painter who tries to earn his living in that particular rat race. But keeping our position as arbiters of painting excellence and as guardians and directors of public taste is of immense importance to us all.

When, in the middle of the eighteenth century, music changed from being a private or courtly amusement and a part of church ceremony to become an entertainment for the great public, the composers of music began to exercise the office of music critic in the public press. And naturally they did it better than anyone else because they knew what music was really about. The list of composers who were also music critics is very large — Wagner, Schumann, Debussy, Berlioz, and many others; in our day, Aaron Copland, Virgil Thomson, Paul Bowles, Henri Sauguet, and so on. When the enjoyment of music had become a public matter it was very important to the musical profession that the public be kept informed by the people who actually knew about it — the composers who wrote the pieces.

Until now painting has always been a private affair between the painter and his clients. No public was involved. When the public had to be informed about something, it was told either by the scholar or professor, if it concerned art of the past or, if it were a matter of contemporary taste, by the enlightened amateur. For the public was merely being notified about something that had already taken place.

The enlightened amateur, of course, has no professional standing and no real knowledge. True, he must have taste. And, just as flair is the ability to predict the present, taste is the ability to predict the past — to know in advance which past style or object will please. Nevertheless, the possession of taste, though it infers a knowledge of past styles, implies in no way any sense or knowledge whatever about contemporary art. Nor does the enlightened amateur have any responsibility to the professional body of painters. At the most he is a journalist, and as such can always correct in tomorrow's edition, if he is forced to, the errors he has made in today's. Dealing with any contemporary painting matter, he is notoriously prejudiced, venal, or inaccurate. Sometimes all three.

None of this has any importance whatever as long as the painter is dealing directly with a private client. Voice and act are always more convincing than the printed word. But if his exploiters — the poets and art appreciation — actually succeed in forcing painting into the public domain, and by the dissemination of false culture and half education bewitch away the painter's cli-

ents, the painter will be forced to do what the
composer did before him — take his pen in hand.
There is no reason why the painter cannot. He has
all the conviction of the man who knows. And
anyone can teach him to spell.

So now the painter has lost his guild. Although
his loss has gained him a great personal liberty, it
has deprived him of much greater things — he is
poor, lives in an ugly world, has more trouble
getting his training, and must paint smaller pictures. But perhaps, nevertheless, it is just as well
that the painter has no defense, no organization,
and no creed. For now he is not really vulnerable
anywhere. His profession has nothing more to
lose. In the difficult times to come, his alone of all
the professions will probably manage to survive
and to continue its work of re-creating the world.

Everything else in our world is built on organization, or technological progress, or on both, and
these are the most vulnerable things there are. The
greater and more complicated an organization,
the more easily it can be destroyed by even a pre-
liminary Armageddon. And nothing but an act of
God can stop technological progress. That must
continue to grow till, like the dinosaur, it crushes
itself by its own mass — and us with it. Examples
are innumerable. Let us take the films.

In the early days the movies' tools were simple
and their expenses were light. Films were enormously amusing to make. It was not necessary for

every picture to be a success. The cost of a failure
made in doing something perhaps new and interesting could be charged against the profit made on
the success of something else, possibly also new
and interesting. So the films had great variety, were
full of invention, and came in all sizes and shapes
for all needs and tastes.

Technological progress brought in the talkies.
These cost a great deal more to make. Box-office
failures were too expensive to be risked. The sure-
fire technique of what was later called the soap
opera was early adopted. So also was the exploitation of charm (it was christened sex appeal and
depended on various kittenish ways of not going
to bed) and the depiction of the spending of
money — both infallible comforts for the lonely
and poor, who could be counted on as regular customers for these indifferent opiates. The visual
gags of the wonderful slapstick comedies, which
required the building of elaborate props and the
destruction of lots of property, were replaced by
cheaper verbal gags which involve no invention or
expense whatever, but only insult. Even with all
these economies, companies frequently went into
a carefully concealed receivership.

With Technicolor, film became too expensive
even to cut. Continuity, which of course can be
got only by considerable cutting and waste, became so vague that it now confuses even the habitual moviegoer himself, accustomed as he is to
supply the missing sequence out of his memory of

similar pictures. The only happy men in Hollywood are the camera men and technological ex-
perts — just as the only people happy about the
atomic bomb (the physicists who made it possible
are appalled) are the engineers who devised that
alarming gadget. The movie makers themselves,
the producers, directors, writers, designers, and
musicians, all the best talent that can be assembled
and who are now made to do a job that is infinitely beneath their capabilities, are bored to a
guilty inferiority and a hopeless despair by this too
easy routine of pleasing. And now television.

They have held it off for ten or fifteen years.
They cannot hold it off any longer. Technological
progress must prevail. But to feed even two major
networks — twice twenty-four hours of new images every day — the industry must unthinkably
expand and enormously debase its product, and get
paid for it, no longer by the harassed but willing
citizen who pursues in a dark and intra-uterine
comfort his dreams of love and money, but by the
manufacturer, who will pass these astronomical
miles of film on to his own public — a small piece
of ham in the sandwich of his publicity. And this
manufacturer will prove a more doubtful, difficult, unwilling, and conservative censor than even
the famous eleven-year-old girl whose limits of experience and comprehension are the standards for
today's censorship. The whole industry envisages
the future with anxiety, even with terror. And
well it may. I am sure that Æsop's fable is wrong,

and that the frog does not intend to puff himself up as big as the bull. He only wishes to be a mite more imposing, to improve his appearance just a little. But once he has swallowed technological progress there is no stopping. He must swell till he pops.

The painter, alone of all the modern world, has no part in all this — no organization to lose, no dependence on science or speculation or philosophy. It is one to him whether he lives in a relativistic or a Fortian universe. His profession is the one conservative force in our civilization, securely based on seeing-is-believing, and he is soundly occupied in seeing what is before his own nose. He has nothing to do with technological progress or with mass production, for he has nothing to do with the interchangeable units and the precise measurements on which they are both built (even though I have read somewhere that one of the promises of television in Technicolor is that it will bring modern pictures in natural colors into every home). He uses nothing that is of any consequence to him that is not at least five centuries old. He even refuses to paint by electric light. He can do without modern pigments or manufacture them himself. He can paint a picture with materials found in the most primitive household, make brushes out of goose feathers and his wife's old fur piece if he must, and paint out of mud from the ditch. The literary man needs the printing press and universal literacy; the composer, the familiar musical instruments and their trained executants. The painter alone can view with complete composure the probable extinction of Western culture. For he knows that with the simplest rules of honesty, cookery, and observation, he can build up another one, and for himself at any rate, every bit as good.

PRINTER'S NOTE

This book is set on the Linotype in GRANJON, *a type named in compliment to Robert Granjon, type-cutter and printer — 1523–1590, Antwerp, Lyons, Rome, Paris. Granjon, the boldest and most original designer of his time, was one of the first to practice the trade of type-founder apart from that of printer.*

Linotype GRANJON *was designed by George W. Jones, who based his drawings upon a face used by Claude Garamond (1510–1561) in his beautiful French books.* GRANJON *more closely resembles Garamond's own type than do any of the various modern faces that bear his name.*

The book was composed, printed, and bound by The Plimpton Press, Norwood, Massachusetts. The typography of this volume, the drawing on the title page, and the binding design are by W. A. Dwiggins.